Lessons from
My Good Old Boat

By the same author

A Cruising Guide to New Jersey Waters

Dictionary of Nautical Acronyms and Abbreviations

Lessons from
My Good Old Boat

DONALD LAUNER

Sheridan House

This edition published 2007 by
Sheridan House Inc.
145 Palisade Street
Dobbs Ferry, NY 10522
www.sheridanhouse.com

Library of Congress Cataloging-in-Publication Data
Launer, Donald
    Lessons learned from my good old boat / Donald Launer.
        p. cm.
    Includes bibliographical references and index.
    ISBN 978-1-57409-250-9 (pbk. : alk. paper)
    1. Sailing. 2. Yachting. I. Title.

GV811.L33 2007
797.124—dc22   2007023910

ISBN 13: 978-1-57409-250-9
ISBN 10: 1-57409-250-2

Printed in the United States of America

Contents

Electronics

Navigation and Boathandling

Engines and Accessory Equipment

CONTENTS

Foreword

It is a true pleasure working with Don Launer as a member of the *Good Old Boat* team. His articles go back almost to our first issue, since it was very early on that he discovered us. We recognized immediately the great value of Don's contributions and made him a contributing editor without having met him in person.

Later, we did meet at a boat show, and some time after that we spent several days with Don when we decided to feature this very competent sailor and the boat he built from a bare hull. The story of Don and DELPHINUS appears in our January 2006 issue.

Within an hour spent aboard DELPHINUS, my husband and magazine co-founder, Jerry Powlas, fell deeply in love with Don's Lazy Jack 32. This is a boat which sails as it should and is set up and outfitted as one should be for minimal effort and maximum sailing. From bow to stern, DELPHINUS is a clear testament to Don's skills as a craftsman and sailor.

The great many articles he has prepared for *Good Old Boat* also speak volumes (if you'll pardon the pun) about Don's ability to communicate the knowledge he has gained over many decades spent sailing. And they say even more about the breadth and depth of this sailor. He is a master in every way, and we're delighted to offer a regular forum for Don Launer and his nautical talents.

This collection of the articles he has written over the years, mostly but not solely for *Good Old Boat*, makes the scope of his experience evident. Upon thumbing through this book, you are likely to ask, "Is there any nautical theme Don hasn't yet addressed?"

We hope the answer will be, "Yes," although we have the same nagging doubts you do. If, after a lifetime of sailing and boatbuilding, he has left nothing out of this collection of his work, however, what remains for the next issue of *Good Old Boat* and the one after that? As you enjoy this book, think of this as one collection which will eventually need an update. Like all good old boats, it is a work in progress. We hope DELPHINUS has many more lessons in store for Captain Don Launer.

Karen Larson
Founder and Editor of *Good Old Boat Magazine*

Acknowledgments

Most of the illustrations and photographs are my own, however I must gratefully acknowledge the illustrations that were provided by Ted Tollefson, with whom I have worked while preparing our *101* series together. These *101* articles appear in each issue of *Good Old Boat Magazine*.

The Facnor Company and Yanmar have graciously given permission for the use of their illustrations.

Without these generous contributions this book would have been diminished.

Finally, I'd like to thank Karen Larson and Jerry Powlas, founders and editors of *Good Old Boat Magazine*, for their encouragement and support for this project.

Introduction

Today, most of us find that there seems to be less free time than there was a generation ago, and putting aside time to read a book has become more and more difficult. With an anthology format, however, an article, complete within itself, can be selected at random and be read in five to fifteen minutes (or a bit longer if you tend to ruminate on new ideas as I do). This is a great advantage for time-starved readers.

This book is a compilation, or anthology, of some of the hundreds of articles I have written over the years. Most of them originally appeared in *Good Old Boat Magazine*, for which I am Contributing Editor. Others were published in *Cruising World, SAIL,* and *Offshore* magazines.

These articles are grouped together in categories, or chapters, such as *Sails and Rigging* or *Electronics*, and each of the articles under these broad headings cover separate subjects. Thus, in the chapter titled *The Environment* are such diverse topics as *Our Magnetic Earth* and *Shipworms*, and each of these articles stands on its own.

Many of these articles, which previously appeared in boating magazines, have been updated and supplemented with additional material.

Sails and Rigging

Mainsail Furling
and Reefing

When the wind suddenly picks up, or a squall-line is approaching, the ability to douse the sails, or reduce sail area quickly, efficiently, and safely, is vital. If you're sailing solo, shorthanded, or you are handicapped, this important job can be particularly difficult and dangerous. Of course there are high-tech hydraulic and electrical systems that can accomplish this, but for the average sailor, it has to be done manually by either furling or reefing the sails by hand.

Furling means to roll up, or gather, a lowered sail, and tie it to prevent it from blowing in the wind.

Reefing means to reduce the area of a sail, allowing the boat to continue sailing under heavier wind conditions.

Reefing can be accomplished by many of the same methods used for furling, as long as the reefing gear has been designed to take the loads of a partially furled (reefed) sail.

There are several ways of reefing a mainsail:

Jiffy or slab reefing

This is the most traditional type of mainsail reefing system. The sail has one or more horizontal lines of *reef points*. To reef, the lower part of the sail, up to the reef points, is brought down to the boom by means of cringles on the luff and leech of the mainsail. Lines through these cringles (*earings*, or *reefing pendants*) are used to pull the luff and the leech of the mainsail down to boom level. This can be accomplished with two separate lines or with a single reefing line. Alternately, the luff can be pulled down manually

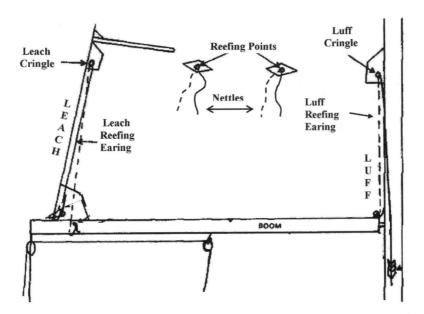

A fully-raised mainsail with jiffy or slab reefing

and the luff cringle put on a hook at the gooseneck fitting (if the hook has a compound curve, it's called a *ram's horn*). Then, the unused portion of the sail (the *bunt*) is tied around the boom using reefing lines on the sail (*nettles*). These lines pass through the horizontal line of reinforced grommets (*reefing points*) and hang down on each side of the sail. The earings, or reefing pendants, that pull the luff and leech of the sail down to the boom take most of the load on the sail, with the nettles merely confining the reefed portion of the sail. Generally, the sail sets better if you use jiffy or slab reefing than most other types of reefing systems.

Vertical in-mast mainsail reefing

Rolling the mainsail up inside the mast requires a specially-designed mast and roller system, which means a substantial investment if this system is retrofitted onto an existing boat. Vertical or horizontal roller reefing for mainsails makes reducing sail much faster and easier for the shorthanded or solo sailor. The trade-off for vertical reefing is more weight aloft (higher center of gravity) even when the sail is furled, and increased windage, due

4

to the larger mast extrusion. This system also requires a flatter-cut mainsail without a normal roach and battens (although vertical battens are sometimes used). This reduces the mainsail area and efficiency. As with all "in the spar" roller-reefing systems, there is the possibility of a jam, which is usually due to operator error.

Vertical aft-mast mainsail reefing

This system rolls the mainsail up on a spar just aft of the mast, and thus can often be adapted to an existing mast; however a new mainsail will be required. As with in-mast reefing, a sail with a roach and battens cannot be used, and the furled sail creates more weight aloft and increased windage.

Vertical retrofitted in-mast mainsail reefing

This system uses an additional aluminum extrusion, in which the mainsail is roller-reefed. This extrusion is riveted to the aft side of the mast. This necessitates a new mainsail and also usually requires a new boom, or one that is modified. The problems of added weight aloft and windage, as well as a special flatter-cut mainsail with no roach or battens, still exist.

Horizontal rotating boom mainsail reefing

In this system, the sail is rolled up on a rotating boom. This requires a specially-designed boom and gooseneck. On smaller sailboats, the boom is manually pulled out of a spring-loaded gooseneck and rotated as necessary. On larger boats heavier, geared equipment is necessary to rotate the boom.

If the mainsheet block is not located at the extreme end of the boom, then a fitting called a *boom claw, reefing claw,* or *claw ring* must be used. This fitting encircles the boom and rolled-up sail like a claw. It is open at the top to allow room for the hoisted part of the sail, with rollers around this top opening, and an eye at the bottom, to which the mainsheet block is attached.

One of the disadvantages of rotating boom reefing is that the sail's luff rope builds up around the forward end of the boom if more than a couple of rotations are made. In addition, there is no clew outhaul, allowing the clew to creep forward. Also, as more turns are taken, the more the end of the boom droops. However, the weight and windage aloft are as low as with a conventional rig, and the sail can have a roach and battens (if the battens are horizontal).

Horizontal in-boom mainsail reefing

With in-the-boom reefing, the mainsail is rolled up on a roller inside the boom's special extrusion. The added weight and windage aloft are much less than with a vertical roller reefing system, and the sail can have a roach, as with rotating boom reefing. With this type of reefing system the mainsheet block location is not the problem that it is with a rotating boom system, but there is still the lack of a clew outhaul. An advantage of this system is that, should there be a jam, the mainsail can still be lowered, an option that is sometimes impossible with an in-mast jam.

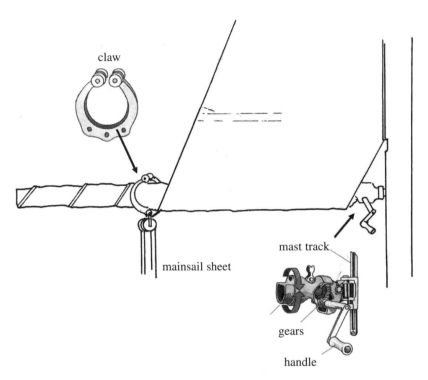

claw

mainsail sheet

mast track

gears

handle

The parts of a rotating boom reefing system

Whichever system is selected, it's important that you and your crew practice reefing or furling under ideal conditions, since a white-knuckles blow is not the best time to learn.

Roller Reefing and Furling Jibs

The ability to furl or reef the headsails efficiently and safely is vital.

Furling means to completely drop, roll up, or gather, a lowered sail, and tie it to prevent it from blowing in the wind.

Reefing means reducing the area of a sail, allowing the boat to continue sailing under increasing wind conditions.

Reefing can be accomplished by many of the same methods used for furling, that is, if the reefing gear has been designed to take the loads of a partially furled (reefed) sail.

Headsails are those sails that are ahead of the most forward mast(s). These may be *staysails*, such as jibs, that are fastened to a *stay*, usually the forestay, or headsails such as spinnakers which, since they are not fastened to the forestay, are headsails but not staysails.

Hanked-on (traditional) foresails

The traditional luff system for staysails is a flexible wire or rope luff with snap-shackles that are used to attach ("hank") it to the forestay. This allows the jib to be fastened to the forestay before raising it, and also to stay attached when it is being lowered.

Hanked-on jibs vary in size. The smallest is the storm or spitfire jib. Working jibs are often given numbers, depending on their size, such as a "No. 2 Jib," or a "No. 3 Jib," with a "No. 1 Jib" being the largest. When a jib is large enough to overlap the mast, it is called a genoa jib, or just a genoa, after Genoa, Italy, where it was first introduced by a Swedish sailing team.

The advantage of a hanked-on headsail is that the luff is attached to the forestay, which is strong and relatively rigid. In addition, this type of sail can be constructed to its optimum shape. The downside is that in deteriorating conditions, when a smaller jib must be substituted, working on the foredeck is hazardous, especially on a boat that is shorthanded or solo-sailed. The severe heeling, rapid vertical accelerations, and spray or solid water coming over the bow creating a slippery deck are not the most pleasant conditions in which to try to lower or change the headsail.

Roller furling on the luff-wire

The first roller-furling headsails were rolled up on their own luff-wire, just behind the forestay, and were not, technically, a staysail. With this roller-furling system, the foot of the luff is attached to a deck mounted drum and the head is attached to the halyard, through a swivel aft of the forestay. Thus, the headsail can be furled from the cockpit, without going onto the foredeck. But the tension required on the halyard to reduce unwanted sagging of the center of the headsail is enormous. This sag also creates a poor sail-shape, and that early system was shunned by racing sailors. In addition, the furling line on the roller drum had to be wound in one direction so that the forces that would cause twisting of the wire would tighten the lay of the wire rather than open up the lay. Also, a fitting usually has to be installed that prevents the head of the sail from wrapping itself around the forestay. With this type of furling, reefing is not practical, except in very light winds, or for a short time when approaching a mooring, dock, or slip. Although this system is seldom used today, roller gear is still available.

Roller furling on a foil

It wasn't long before rolling a jib up on its own luff-wire was replaced with a grooved foil, which enclosed the forestay. The sail's luff-rope, or bolt-rope, is fed into the groove of this foil, which has swivels at the bottom of the roller drum and at the top of the foil. With this system the headsail can be rolled up around the foil and, since it is on the forestay, sag is no greater than with traditional hanked-on jibs. This system can accommodate a working jib, genoa, and even a large gennaker or Code-Zero. With the added rigidity of the forestay and foil, it becomes practical to reef a larger headsail, resulting in fewer required headsail changes. In addition to adding convenience, these foils have provided a more aerodynamically efficient leading edge.

The foils used in roller furling/reefing are also made with a second boltrope groove, which allows changing headsails without losing the power of the headsail during the change—a boon to the high-performance enthusiasts as well as the cruising sailor.

Although roller-reefing jibs can be partially rolled up, they lose efficiency when rolled up more than about 15%-20% and the tension on the roller system becomes severe. In high wind conditions, the center of effort

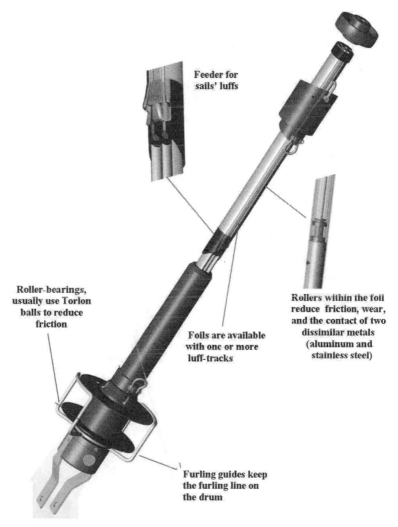

Feeder for sails' luffs

Roller-bearings, usually use Torlon balls to reduce friction

Rollers within the foil reduce friction, wear, and the contact of two dissimilar metals (aluminum and stainless steel)

Foils are available with one or more luff-tracks

Furling guides keep the furling line on the drum

A roller furling system, *courtesy of Facnor*

of a partially furled roller jib is high off the deck as compared to a storm jib—something that doesn't help the situation as the winds increase.

There is no replacement for a proper storm jib under really bad conditions.

Rotating the foil to furl or reef the sail can be done in several ways. Most often it is with a single line that is wound around a drum at the base of the foil. This line leads back to the cockpit. It can also be done with a "continuous line," that is, with a loop of line that leads back to the cockpit. This continuous line wraps around a large diameter drum which is supposed to be lighter, stronger, and safer than the traditional single-line drum system.

One advantage of the continuous line system is that since there is no drum at the base of the sail to store the furling line, the headsail can be several inches closer to the deck. In lieu of manually roller furling the headsail, there are also electric or hydraulic systems available, with a motor at the base of the foil, replacing the drums of the manual systems. Most of these electric or hydraulic furlers have a winch-handle socket or a continuous line manual backup system in case of electric, hydraulic, or mechanical failure.

The continuous line furling system, *courtesy of Facnor*

The installation of many roller furlers requires the forestay to be cut during installation, which means a new terminal or a whole new forestay. Some manufacturers provide roller systems that can be installed without cutting the existing stay. The size of the furling system will depend on the length of the forestay and its wire diameter.

Modern furling systems are reliable and easy to use, and are increasingly finding their way aboard cruising, as well as racing, sailboats.

The Club-Footed Jib

I'm alone in the cockpit of my schooner DELPHINUS, short-tacking up a narrow section of the bay. Half aloud I say to myself, "Ready about. Hard alee." I remain seated by the wheel as the bow comes up through the wind. The club-footed jib swings over, then the foresail changes sides and finally the mainsail follows over to the new tack. I think of all the years I have spent sailing without the luxury of cruising with everything self-tending. Sometimes I feel a bit guilty, as if I should be doing something.

What is a club-footed jib?

Many sailors have never encountered the club-footed jib and are unfamiliar with its operation. With an understanding of the theory and terminology behind the basic jib boom system, it should be obvious that the club-footed jib is truly an underestimated headsail for the cruising sailor. Basically, the club-footed jib is a non-overlapping headsail set on a boom. The sail itself has a sailcloth weight and clew height similar to a normal headsail. The sail is fastened to the boom loose-footed, with only the clew of the sail attached to the after end of the boom. The boom has a gooseneck fitting at its forward end, so it is free to move horizontally and vertically. The gooseneck is attached either directly to the forestay or to a pedestal just aft, the latter being the optimal system, in my experience. The placement of the pedestal aft of the sail's tack automatically allows the sail to become fuller when it is eased out on a broad reach or run. This is more aerodynamically efficient than if the boom were attached to the forestay, which would make the sail flat on all points of wind unless the clew were retrimmed (Fig. 1).

11

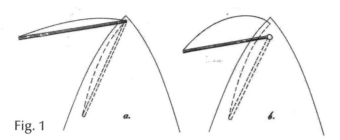

Fig. 1

Pedestal mount

The advantage of the pedestal mount was disputed by world voyager Eric Hiscock in his book, *Cruising Under Sail*. His contention is that such a method causes the belly of the sail to move too far aft, and the upper part of the sail to lose efficiency when the boom lifts. I have never observed this problem and tend to follow the recommendations of other experts such as Jeremy Howard-Williams who, in his authoritative book *Sails*, stresses the importance of mounting the jib boom on a pedestal aft of the forestay.

As shown in Figure 1, the system provides the headsail with a built-in whisker pole for downwind work, without the pole's inherent disadvantages in handling.

Although not generally used today, in years past the fullness and shape of the eased club-footed jib could be controlled by adjusting the pedestal fore and aft (Figure 2). The equipment to do this consisted of one or two rods, used as tracks, fitted with a sliding gooseneck fitting to which the boom was attached. Various names were used for this arrangement. In Gloucester, "boom horse" was usual. "Boom rider" and "horse rider" were other labels.

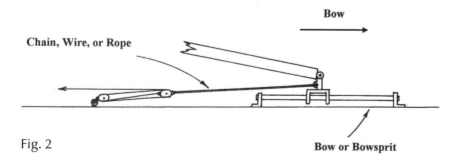

Fig. 2

Fig. 3

Raising and lowering sail

With the headsail hanked to the forestay in the normal manner, and the clew securely fastened to the boom's aft end, we now have encountered our first potential problem: The lower part of the sail cannot be lowered down the stay. Because the sail will not stretch and is attached to the clew and luff, it will not pass a perpendicular line between the clew and the forestay unless one of several measures is taken. Figure 3 illustrates the problem.

This can be done in several ways:

1. Unsnap the lower hanks from the forestay.
2. Loosen the clew from the jib boom.
3. Use a short jib boom, unattached to the deck or forestay, that rides forward as the halyard is eased off. (Figure 4).
4. Fasten the lower jib hanks to an artificial stay (called a "jackstay" or "relieving line") that automatically becomes slack when the sail is lowered, allowing the luff to move aft.

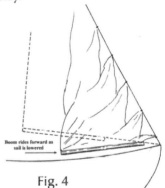

Fig. 4

Artificial headstay

Solution #4 is the most practical. The relieving line is attached to the luff of the jib, as depicted in Figure 5a. The other end of the relieving line is fastened to the tack of the sail so that with the jib raised it is under tension, providing an artificial forestay.

Figure 5b shows that as the jib halyard is eased and

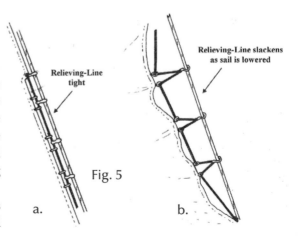

Fig. 5

a.   b.

13

the upper part of the jib drops down the stay, the relieving line becomes slack enough to allow the lower sail luff to move aft, allowing that section to be lowered.

The jib sheet

The self-tending aspect of the club-footed jib is accomplished with a car for the jib sheet. The sheet is led from multiple-part purchase on the traveler car through a block on the boom's aft end, then to a block on the forward end, and finally back to the cockpit (Figure 6). Leading the

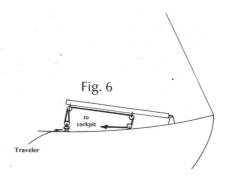

Fig. 6

jib sheet forward before going aft to the cockpit is necessary to prevent the pull on the jib sheet from restricting the athwartship movement of the traveler car. The foredeck traveler track should be wide enough so that the jib sheet has enough athwartship travel to prevent backwinding of the mainsail (or in the case of a schooner, the foresail). This usually requires a track that stretches nearly from rail to rail, and is a potential hazard on the foredeck. Recessing the track into the deck, while seldom done, is one solution. Being aware of the hazard and avoiding it is another.

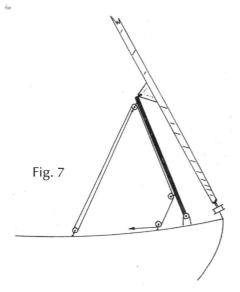

Fig. 7

Roller furling

Roller furling may be used in conjunction with the boom headsail and is as easily adaptable as with a conventional headsail. One method of roller furling (that ultimately will present multiple problems and is therefore unsatisfactory) leaves the clew of the sail fastened to the boom's end. When the sail is rolled up, the boom rises vertically off the deck (Figure 7).

Better rig

A far better rig is shown in Figure 8. The drum furling line remains standard. The clew outhaul line, however, is routed through a sheave on the boom's aft end, then forward to the pedestal, then back to the cockpit in the normal manner. With the sail unfurled and the clew outhaul belayed, the self-tending feature of the club-footed jib remains unaltered.

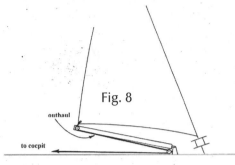

Fig. 8

Lazyjacks

Although considered archaic to many, lazyjacks, when used on a club-footed jib, can be a fine asset. This is especially true when the headsail is set on a bowsprit. This allows strolls along the clear bowsprit to hand a jib that is already under control and not spilling onto the walk area. Lazyjacks also provide the additional advantage of serving as a jib boom topping lift, so that the boom will not fall onto the deck when the headsail is lowered.

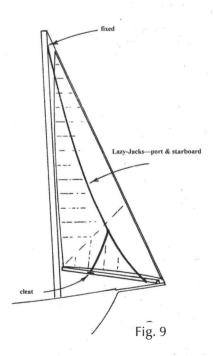

Fig. 9

There are several different ways to rig jib boom lazyjacks. Figure 9 shows one method. An alternative method calls for the lower section of the lazyjack to be fixed, with the upper section led through a mast-head block and down to the deck, as done with many topping lifts. My preference, due to rigging simplicity, is the method shown in Figure 9. Once adjusted and in place, further adjustments of the lazyjack are infrequent.

Downhaul line

Another important item used with club-footed jibs is the jib downhaul. When turning up into the wind to drop the jib, the club foot naturally tends to swing across the foredeck. Trying to lower the jib under these conditions invites a smack on the shin even under mild sea conditions, which doesn't make for pleasant sailing. A jib downhaul line, led from the jibhead cringle, down through a block at the tack and aft along the deck, allows the jib to be pulled down from well aft of the swinging boom. Once down, the jib boom can be secured in a fixed position on deck. Some prefer to secure the aft end of the boom with a short halyard to the mainmast, others like to fasten the boom to a port or starboard lifeline, leaving the foredeck clear. It is generally not wise to lead the downhaul line through the jib hanks; even though the line is of small diameter, there tends to be a binding problem. For those who prefer not to see the downhaul line blowing free in the wind when the jib is up, small lanyards, or "lizards" may be used at several intervals along the luff of the sail to keep the downhaul line shipshape (Figure 10).

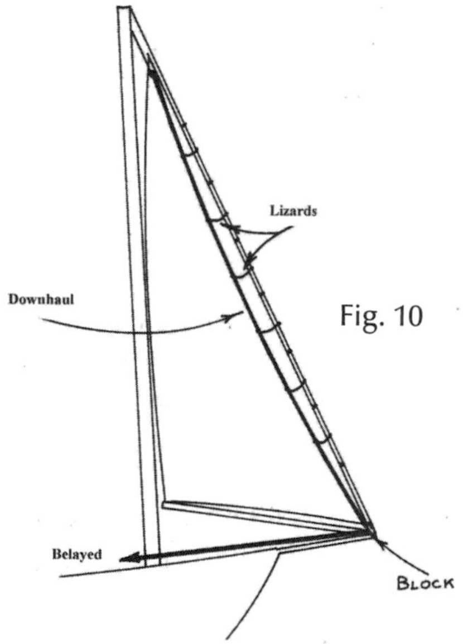

Fig. 10

Those are the basics of the club-footed jib. At first it may seem overly complicated, but it is in fact designed to remove complications and in practice becomes very simple. The convenience for the short-handed cruising sailor of sailing with a self-tending rig has to be experienced to be appreciated.

A group of sailing friends, who frequently join me aboard my schooner, have come up with a routine that tells the whole story. At the command, "Ready about; hard alee," all the seated guests stamp their feet as if wildly running about.

They say it sounds more like a racing boat.

Standing Rigging

Standing rigging is the term given to the cables that support a sailboat's mast(s), the forestay, backstay, and shrouds, as well as specialized cables such as the bobstay, the boomkin stay, and triatic stay. *Standing* indicates a fixed cable that stands in place and does not move, as opposed to *running* rigging, which is used to hoist sails and runs over the sheaves in blocks.

In the early days of the square-riggers the masts were held up with tarred hemp, one of the earliest types of standing rigging. Later, galvanized, multi-strand iron cable, and then steel, known as *wire rope*, replaced the hemp, and much later stainless steel became the standing rigging of choice.

The fittings at each end of the standing rigging, which attach the standing rigging to the mast or hull, are known as terminals, end terminals, or end fittings.

The requirements for standing rigging are strength and minimal stretch. Flexibility is not a major factor as it is with running rigging. Since it must also be able to resist corrosion, stainless steel is the most common standing rigging for recreational vessels.

In marine applications, stainless steel is an alloy of steel, chromium, and nickel, and is identified with a 300-series designation. Types 302 and 304 are widely used for rigging and fasteners. Type 302 is a general purpose stainless steel, resistant to many corrosives, with good strength. The 304 sub-alloy is formulated for specific applications.

By adding 2% molybdenum to 304 you get 316, which has the best corrosion resistance among standard stainless steels, and is particularly resistant to salt water corrosion. However 316 is only about 85% as strong as 302 and 304. Standing rigging of type 316 will generally outlive 302 and 304, especially in tropical climates, but the wire size may have to be increased, which also results in larger turnbuckles, jaws, eyes, clevis pins, etc.

Wire rope is identified by the diameter of the cable; the number of strands (bundles) of wire, and the number of individual wires in each bundle; the type of wire material; and the core. This core can be either wire or fiber. A fiber core wire rope is often used in running rigging. The core is saturated with oil, which helps to lubricate the individual wires as they slide against each other while making their turns around sheaves. Wire-core cable is primarily used for standing rigging.

For running rigging, flexibility is important. Typical for running rigging wire rope would be 7 x 19, in which there are 7 bundles of wire with 19 individual wires in each bundle.

Since flexibility is not the important factor in standing rigging, the typical wire rope for standing rigging is the 1 x 19, which indicates 19 wires in a single bundle.

The correct way to measure the diameter of wire rope

The cross-section of a wire rope should have as much metal and as few voids as possible. Rod rigging has no voids, and the Dyform 1 x 7, where each of the 7 wires is extruded through a special die to produce a shape that reduces these voids, comes in a close second for strength.

Although it would seem that the standing rigging should be as large as possible, increasing the diameter of the wire rope beyond the designer's specifications leads to increased windage and weight aloft.

Standing rigging rarely breaks in the middle of its span; about 99% of standing rigging failures occur close to the terminal fittings, with the

The incorrect way to measure the diameter of wire rope

18

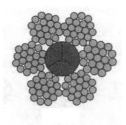

A 6 x 19 fiber-cored wire rope used for running rigging

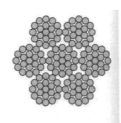

The 7 x 19 is the most commonly used wire rope for running rigging.

The less flexible 1 x 19 is the most commonly used wire rope for standing rigging.

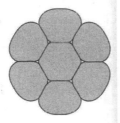

The 1 x 7 Dyform wire rope, used for standing rigging, increases the amount of steel in a given cross-section.

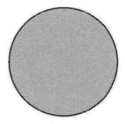

Rod-rigging is the strongest standing rigging for a given diameter, but has some drawbacks.

bottom fitting the major culprit. Usually the first indication will be a broken strand. Toggles should be used at the terminal fittings to correct any misalignment and reduce this possibility. For the cruising sailboat, a coil of 1 x 19 wire and some swageless fittings, such as Norseman or Sta-Lok, make replacing that failing piece of rigging an easy job, with just the use of hand tools. Rod rigging, on the other hand, gives few advance signs of a failure, and makes emergency repairs more difficult.

Inspecting standing rigging for broken wires, or meat-hooks, is best done using a cotton ball and running it down the cable. If fingers are used you'll find that these meat-hooks cut like a razor blade. When a broken wire is found, that cable should be replaced immediately, and it's a very likely indication that the other cables of the same age are in similar condition.

With rod rigging there is little that can be done by the boat owner to determine the rod's condition (short of an X-ray)—and one good snag on a piling while docking can mean the end of that rod.

Another location that should be checked regularly with all rigging is where the upper shroud bends around the tip of the spreader. There is an additional problem here, since this is usually also the point where two dissimilar metals meet. With rod rigging, this bend around the spreader and the special fitting used should be done by a professional rigger.

There is no rule as to when standing rigging has to be replaced. The standing rigging on boats used in fresh water will last longer than boats in salt water, and in the salt waters of the semi-tropics many riggers suggest replacing the standing rigging every 10 years.

For preventive maintenance the standing rigging should be rinsed off from as high as possible at the end of the day, especially after sailing with salt spray coming over the bow.

Terminal Fittings for Standing Rigging

The stainless steel standing rigging that holds up our masts is critical to our sailing safety, and the terminals at the end of these stainless steel cables are the vital connection between those cables and the mast tangs or the hull's chain-plates. Although most of us are only familiar with a single terminal type, the swaged fitting, there are actually many other types of standing rigging terminals.

In the old sailing ships, standing rigging was natural-fiber rope, terminating in an eye, which was wrapped around a wood deadeye. When metallurgy was finally able to produce strong and flexible wire cable, these natural rope shrouds were replaced by wire rope, but deadeyes still were used for tensioning. Finally, as manufacturing technology advanced further, stainless steel standing rigging and threaded turnbuckles superseded the ancient ways of supporting masts.

There still are, however, some boats whose stainless steel rigging terminates in an eye. This eye is usually a wire-rope splice around a thimble—a sailor's art that is not in the repertoire of most of today's boaters.

The wire-rope splice around an eye is seldom seen today

Once the eye is formed at the end of the shroud, turnbuckles can then be attached to this eye/thimble combination at the hull end and shackles at the upper ends. Although a wire splice is the strongest way to create this eye, occasionally you'll find "bulldog" fittings used. These fittings are U-shaped clamps with a sliding bar, which is usually curved to fit the wire-rope diameter.

The *bulldog* fitting

Though seldom seen as a working system today, these bulldog fitting clamps are useful for an emergency repair of a broken shroud. When used for this purpose, the U-shaped end should never be used on the standing part of the shroud, since it tends to crush the cable. Even if you never plan to use this method, it's a good idea to have two or three bulldog clamps and a thimble, sized to your standing rigging, as part of your emergency kit. Galvanized bulldog clamps can be purchased from your local hardware store for less than a dollar each, and stainless steel ones are available in marine stores for a few dollars each. With these you can rapidly make a relatively strong eye at the end of a broken shroud, or connect two broken ends together. This is a much faster quick-fix than trying to use a more permanent fitting, such as a Nicropress, since the oval sleeve of that fitting requires a cleanly cut wire end, which could take time to accomplish—and time is in short supply during an emergency.

Getting a clean cut on stainless wire rope is a tough job unless you've spent a lot of money for a pair of cable cutters made just for that purpose. Instead, you can achieve a clean cut with a hacksaw and several new, fine-toothed blades. The key to cutting with a hacksaw is to have a portable vise so that you can hold the wire firmly and rotate it as necessary to cut through the strands. A vise-grip will also work in a pinch. Electrical tape, tightly wound around the wire rope at the point of cutting, is a big help.

Another method of creating an eye in wire rope is the Nicropress or Talurit system. This method of terminating the shrouds is occasionally still seen on small boats. An oval metal sleeve is fitted over the short and standing parts of the shroud. This sleeve is then compressed hydraulically or manually, till the relatively soft metal of the sleeve fills in all the voids between the strands of the wire ropes as it compresses them together. To minimize electrolytic action, these sleeves are made of copper or stainless steel when used on stainless steel rigging. The manual Nicropress tool that

The Nicropress fitting

compresses this sleeve looks like a giant bolt-cutter, but instead of cutting blades it has two indentations in the jaws that fit the sleeve. Although some catalogs call this a swaging tool, it should not be confused with real swaging. Another tool for this operation is one which compresses the sleeve between two metal bars by wrenching down two machine screws that pull these bars together. Since it is less effective, this type of tool should only be used on copper sleeves and for non-critical fittings, or as an emergency fix.

The true swaged terminal is the type we are most familiar with. These fittings have an eye, fork, threaded stud, or insulator on one end, and a sleeve, the exact size of the wire rope, on the other. With the wire rope inserted into the fitting's sleeve, the stainless steel sleeve is hydraulically squeezed, rolled, or pounded till it forms into the contours of the wire rope. The roller swager, sometimes called a Kearney, after the manufacturer, has two sets of wheels that compress the terminal onto the wire. This system can be used for wire up to about ¼". Larger wire sizes require a swaging machine, an enormous device that can weigh a ton or more. It hammers the fitting until the sleeve is beaten into the wire. This machine, which costs thousands of dollars, performs the most satisfactory swaging operation.

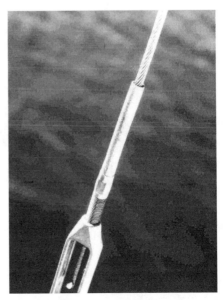

The *swaged* fitting

Most wire terminals found on today's sailboats are swaged fittings; but Master Rigger Brion Toss suggests that this is not because they are superior solutions—which they are not—but because these end-fittings can be produced in volume at relatively low prices,

Various manufacturers market the *swageless* fitting

and fastening them to the rigging can be done rapidly by anyone with the right equipment, whether highly skilled or not. This last point may be the reason for the high number of banana-shaped sleeves on the swaged fittings that Brion encounters on his clients' boats.

There's another type of swaged terminal fitting that looks just like a normal swage fitting, but the sleeve that is squeezed onto the wire is a soft alloy, so that a manual Nicro-Press type tool can be used. This kind of fitting, often used on lifelines, is called a "hand-crimp" fitting. This hand-crimp, soft alloy type of swaged fitting should *not* be used on standing rigging, due to its lesser strength (and I have strong reservations about using it for lifelines, also).

The final terminal fitting is a "swageless" terminal. Although a bit more expensive than the swaged terminal, this fitting is a do-it-yourself terminal that can be connected to the wire rope by the boat owner using just two wrenches.

These fittings are machined from stainless steel and are stronger than any of the other rigging terminals. Because of their strength, reliability, and ease of replacement, they are often the fittings of choice for world voyagers. The fittings are reusable (except for the inner cone) and, as with swaged fittings, are available with an eye, fork, threaded stud, or insulator. There are several manufacturers of this type of terminal: Norseman, Sta-Lok, Suncor, Hi-Mod, and Quick Attach, among others. These swageless fittings are an excellent choice when it comes time to replace the old standing rigging on your boat. It's a job you can do yourself, and one that will create a stronger mast-supporting system than when the boat was new. Installation instructions, with diagrams, come with each fitting.

Winches

In the early history of sail all sailhandling was accomplished through the use of multiple-part block and tackle, or brute strength. From the days of the earliest sailing ships there were, of course, capstans on board, which allowed a stout crew to weigh anchor, and later, in the 19th century, steam-powered anchor-winches came into use aboard larger vessels. But for the recreational sailor it wasn't till the mid 20th century that the sheet and halyard winches, as we now know them, finally came into general use.

Those first expensive winches appeared on the twelve meter boats of the 1950s. Top-of-the-line blocks in those days were made of bronze with no roller bearings, so it was a logical step to construct those first winches of cast bronze also. Those newfangled pieces of equipment were first fabricated for high-end racing yachts and had a maximum of two speeds, without self-tailing.

By the 1970s lighter weight and less expensive winches with aluminum drums appeared on the scene. These could have up to three speeds. Finally, in the 1980s stainless steel drums replaced those of aluminum, and today we can find four speed winches with carbon drums, titanium gears and carbon gearboxes and shafts.

Power ratio

Small winches provide the ability to exert enormous pressures on lines by using a combination of long winch handles, coupled to smaller diameter drums, and ratchets to prevent lines from running free when the pressure is released. Larger winches employ reduction gears and multiple speeds. Whereas the average sailor can exert about a thirty or forty-pound horizontal pull on a line, on larger boats this is just not enough, and sheet pressures in the thousands of pounds are now common on large cruising or racing yachts. By gaining mechanical advantage through leverage (a long winch-handle radius turning a small radius drum), and reduction gears (the number of times the handle is turned to create one revolution of the drum), high "power ratios" can be developed. This power ratio can be simply calculated. It is the handle-to-drum ratio multiplied by the gear ratio. Thus, if you have a 10" handle and 5" drum, and a 5:1 gear ratio, your handle-to-drum ratio is 10/2.5 (2.5 being the radius of the drum), and the mechanical advantage is 4. When this is multiplied by the gear ratio (5) we have a power ratio of 4 x 5 = 20-to-1. Winches are given numbers which approximate this power ratio. Thus, a #8 winch has a power ratio of 8:1. This 8:1 figure is, of course, a theoretical figure, since friction of the internal winch parts and the line on the drum will reduce this ideal number somewhat. With small winches that have no internal gearing, the power ratio is simply the handle-to-drum-radius ratio.

Winch sizes

The smallest of winches are "snubbing" winches. These winches do not have handles. Their advantage is that when a line is tensioned, the winch pawls prevent the drum from rotating which would allow the line to run out again—thus giving the sailor time to prepare for the next pull.

The next size up are single-speed winches with handles. Since these winches have no gears, the mechanical advantage comes through a long winch handle and small drum diameter.

The next higher category consist of those winches that employ gear ratios and multiple speeds. They can multiply a person's arm-power tremendously.

New materials

Since winches are asked to perform under increasingly larger load conditions, the internal gears, bearings and lubrication have also been upgraded to high-tech. In the late 1970s Amoco developed a plastic named Torlon. When used as roller bearings inside a winch, Torlon could take great abuse with little lubrication. Harken immediately seized on this new product and began using it in their winches, however to delay copy-cat use by the competition they called their new roller bearings Duratron, a pseudo name. We now see winches with Torlon bearings becoming standard equipment by nearly all winch manufacturers.

Lubrication

Since modern winches are so reliable, they tend to be the most neglected pieces of gear on board, but just as with everything mechanical, winches require a certain amount of care if they are to perform their job and have an extended life. This care also minimizes the possibility of an unexpected breakdown, and dramatically reduces the physical requirements of the crew.

There are three basic levels of winch maintenance:

1) A fresh water rinse should be done at the end of the sailing day. When you rinse down the topsides, direct the hose at the winches to flush them out and to wash away any saltwater, which degrades the winch grease and corrodes the metals.

Stainless steel, chromed, and anodized aluminum winch drums should be washed regularly, then dried with a cloth. Occasionally, non-abrasive liquid cleaner can be used on stainless steel and chromed winches. Naval jelly, sold by winch manufacturers, can be used on stainless steel drums to remove tarnish and protect the surface. Never use polishes or abrasives to clean the drums of aluminum winches.

2) The second level of maintenance is the "quick check," which will only take about ten or fifteen minutes per winch, and should be done two or three times a season, or more often if the boat is in constant use. Remove the drum from the winch and also remove the main bearings. With a rag moistened with solvent, wipe away grease on exposed surfaces, and examine the winch for wear or damage. Take special note of the condition of the gear teeth and pawls. If there is any indication that the winch is dry, or that the grease in the winch is gummed up and hard, or if you see dirt or sand— then it's time to schedule a winch overhaul immediately.

3) A complete winch overhaul requires taking the winch down to its component parts, cleaning these parts, inspecting for damage, replacing those damaged parts, relubricating, and reassembly. This should be done at least once a year, preferably at the end of the season. Although the first time you do this, the procedure will take a while, due to unfamiliarity, for the typical winch aboard a 30-35 footer, this can be done in about 30-45 minutes. Whenever doing a complete overhaul, especially for the first time, have the manufacturer's diagram of the exploded view of the winch, along

with their service sheet, so that you can follow the recommended lubrication procedure, and be sure that the reassembly will be correct. With this important diagram, you can also identify any parts, by number, that need replacement.

Winch manufacturers supply service manuals for each of their winches, along with kits for routine servicing, which usually include drum screws, pawls, springs, and winch grease. When performing your disassembly be careful that the drum bearings don't stick inside the drum and go overboard. Winches should be lubricated with winch grease, but avoid overgreasing, which can trap salt and water inside the winch. Check the pawls and springs for signs of wear and lubricate them with a light machine oil, such as 3-in-1 or equivalent, rather than grease. Do not grease plastic roller or ball bearings. Winch grease can be purchased at marine supply store, through marine catalogs, and from winch manufacturers. Many winch manufacturers have their own proprietary grease names, such as Lewmar's RaceLube, and others, such as Harken, may recommend a commercially-available product such as Team McLube Sailkote.

With just simple and regular maintenance procedures, your expensive winches can give you decades of reliable service.

Boltrope It On

Ropes are sewn around the edges of sails to distribute the load and prevent tearing. These ropes are called boltropes, and sometimes a more specific name is given, such as luffrope and footrope. In the days of the tall ships, boltropes were always sewn slightly off center, toward the port side of the ship, so that sailors at night could identify the orientation of the sail by feel. Usually sail-track slides are sewn to the luff and foot of a mainsail, but occasionally, usually on small craft, the boltrope itself is fed into the sail track. Although generally more inconvenient, this maximizes the load-distribution on the edge of the sail, as well as becoming more aerodynamically efficient.

When a jib is roller-furling, this luffrope (boltrope) is often fed into the extruded track of the roller-furling system.

Just as when sails are attached to masts, there are occasions on board when you need to fasten other fabric to wood, fiberglass, metal, or some other hard object. Sometimes eyes in the fabric and rope ties do the job, and sometimes stainless steel snaps work, but often this is the time to use the boltrope and track method. This system works especially well under conditions of wind and spray, such as when Sunbrella sides are attached to a hard-top dodger, or when a cockpit canopy needs to be attached to a stainless steel frame.

There is now a modern method of accomplishing this: A preformed boltrope, with a handy sewing tab, is sewn to the edge of the fabric. This boltrope, along with the fabric, can then be fed into the boltrope track, which is fastened to the wood, fiberglass, or metal.

Boltropes, with a sewing tab, come in either Dacron or vinyl. The Dacron boltrope, which is more expensive, has a diameter of $\frac{7}{32}$-inch, and slides easily into the track. It is ideally used in situations where attachment and detachment need to be made quickly and easily or where there are sharp

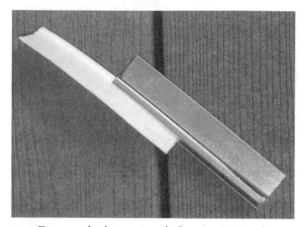

Dacron boltrope and aluminum track

bends in the track. The vinyl boltrope provides a tighter and more waterproof fit, but since it is just slightly larger (¼-inch in diameter) it is more difficult to slide in place, especially around bends, and it cannot be used when the bends are less than a 10-inch radius. The vinyl boltrope is best suited to semi-permanent installations where the track is relatively straight.

The track into which the boltrope slides comes in either extruded PVC or aluminum. The PVC *Flex-a-Rail* is handy when the track needs to have bends in it. For really tight bends the Flex-a-Rail can be softened with steam from a teapot. It is fastened in place with flat-head stainless steel screws or machine-screws, which go through holes drilled in the center of the track. These tracks come in 45-inch lengths, in white, black, or cream.

A heavy-duty PVC track is also available. It has a flange for pan-head screws or bolts and, although much stronger, can only follow gentle bends. It comes in 48-inch lengths, in white.

Anodized aluminum tracks are also available, and come in 48-inch lengths. These tracks are even stronger, but can only be bent in a very large radius. This track also has a mounting flange that will take pan-head screws or bolts. It is best suited for heavy duty jobs, with relatively straight paths.

Vinyl or Dacron boltrope can be attached to the fabric as follows:

"A" shows only one side is finished. This can be used when the other side is not seen.

"B" is used when both sides need to be finished. If the boltrope is used where there is lots of rain or spray, a weather flap can protect the joint.

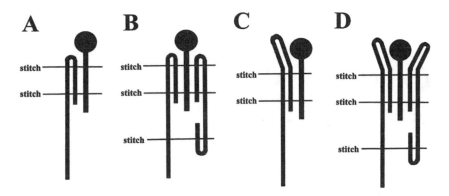

Sewing methods for attaching pre-formed boltrope to canvas

"C" is used when one side of the joint cannot be seen.

"D" is more finished, and provides a waterproof flap to both sides of the boltrope.

Boltropes are also used at the edges of awnings ashore, and in this non-nautical application they are called "awning ropes."

Tracks, boltropes, screws, and other sewing supplies "Awning Tracks and Rope" are available from:

Sailrite Enterprises Inc.
4506 S. State Road 9-57
Churubusco, IN 46723

260.693.2242
800.348.2769
Fax: 260.693.2246
e-mail: sailrite@sailrite.com
web site: www.sailrite.com

The Care and Feeding of Blocks

Blocks, or to use the landlubber's term, pulleys, are as indispensable to the operation of a sailboat as an engine is to a powerboat. They can provide a mechanical advantage or a change in direction of the pull on the fall. Blocks have been around since sailors first hoisted sail, but in the last century the materials as well as the internal parts used to reduce friction have seen a major breakthrough into high-tech. Blocks made of wood were the first to be used, and persisted for two millennia, but they are now seldom seen on today's recreational sailboats—they have been replaced by more modern materials.

Galvanized blocks

In our great-grandparents' day most recreational sailboats used blocks and deck hardware of galvanized iron or steel. They were practical, strong, reasonably long-lasting, and an inexpensive way to set up the running rigging on a sailboat. Today, however, galvanized fittings are seen only on traditional work boats or as dock hardware. Galvanized blocks use a zinc coating to protect the underlying iron or steel from corrosion. Various processes are used to apply the zinc coating. Of all these methods, hot-dip galvanizing, where the iron is immersed in molten zinc, is the most effective, providing a zinc coating of about .003 inch. Less preferable is electroplating, which results in a coating about half as thick. Usually the sheaves of those old blocks were also galvanized and rotated directly on the shaft. Maintenance, in those long-ago times, consisted of an occasional drop of oil.

Bronze blocks

A huge leap forward came when bronze blocks were introduced. Bronze blocks were used on the highest quality yachts from the Civil War to the middle of the 20th century. As late as the 1950s and 1960s, the twelve-meter boats of the America's Cup used bronze blocks and hardware. But even in the mid 1900s, bronze blocks usually lacked bearings for their bronze sheaves. Legendary Nathaniel Herreshoff made cast bronze blocks in six sizes and two styles, and for decades his blocks were top-of-the-line. Bronze was universally considered to be the best material you could use and bronze blocks were used on the finest yachts built for the richest men in the world during this period.

Although bronze was largely replaced by aluminum and stainless steel after the mid 1900s, bronze is now making a strong comeback on both production and custom yachts. This is partly due to the introduction of modern materials as bearings. Bronze has the ability to last almost indefinitely in the marine environment and has several advantages over other materials, such as stainless steel, which is subject to crevice corrosion and rust, or aluminum, which has galvanic surface corrosion problems.

Although the shell of bronze blocks lasts indefinitely, the major problem with early bronze blocks was the plain bronze bearings that wore out and were not easily replaced. This problem has now been largely eliminated and modern bronze-shell blocks make use of roller bearings that reduce the friction to almost zero and there are some bronze blocks where the axles, bearings and sheaves are easily replaceable. These new roller bearings are often made from such modern plastics as Delrin or the better, and more expensive plastic, Torlon. Bearings made from these modern materials have proven to be highly reliable over the last thirty years, and can handle loads equaling the strength of the blocks themselves.

The durability of bronze in the marine environment is indisputable. Bronze artifacts that have lain on the bottom of the sea for over two thousand years show little deterioration. The major problem for the sailor who would like to purchase bronze hardware today is one of quality. A lot of the marine products now being sold as bronze are really brass, with a high zinc and lead content, often cast overseas from scrap metal. This brass alloy is attractive to the manufacturer. It melts at a low temperature and machines like butter. This speeds up the manufacturing process, doesn't wear down the tools and improves the profit margin. It's not a bad product for a pair of candlesticks, but it's a terrible one for important fittings in the marine environment. These brass fittings have a low tensile strength, which decreases even more as dezincification begins, and as the zinc in the alloy turns into acetic zinc-oxide, the resultant white powder attacks wood, causing it to rot. (If you've every noticed wood-rot around your "bronze" fittings, the chances are these fittings aren't really bronze.)

But how are the consumers to tell? Although you would hope that you could rely on the big-name manufacturers that are distributors of "bronze" products, unfortunately many are more profit-oriented than customer-oriented, and their "bronze" is really brass. It's the inevitable result when a manufacturer is more interested in improving their bottom-line than the product to satisfy their customers. Instead of learning how to do things better, they are learning how to do things cheaper and with a higher profit-margin. Of course the consumer could ask whether zinc is used in the manufacturers' alloy, but chances are they couldn't get a straight answer—even if the distributor knew.

This is too bad, since *real* bronze blocks really are maintenance-free (except for of an occasional drop of oil or Teflon spray). You have to sand and varnish wood-shell blocks and stainless-steel blocks tend to bleed rust and are subject to corrosion, but a true bronze block can last the life of the owner—or even the owner's children and grandchildren.

One bronze manufacturer is Roger Winiarski, of Bristol Bronze, in Tiverton, Rhode Island. When Roger, who has over 35 years of experience as a metallurgist, was looking for quality bronze hardware for the restoration of his Herreshoff S-class sloop, he was dismayed to find a lack of quality and a dearth of real-bronze hardware. In order to get what he wanted in style and quality, Roger finally decided he would have to do the casting himself—and thus, in 1989, was born Bristol Bronze. "My philosophy," he says, "is to simply make the best product I can, using the best casting techniques, the best alloys and the best metallurgy. I just hate seeing people turn out less than the best. There is no zinc in my alloys. I use silicon bronze for the majority of my castings, and springs are phosphor bronze."

Bristol Bronze has blocks with bronze sheaves and free-turning bronze axles. The sheaves and axles on these blocks can be replaced by removing the separately-cast cheek-pieces—this might be 20-40 years after the block is put in service. Also, through an agreement with Harken, Bristol Bronze can now supply blocks with Harken sheaves that have Torlon roller bearings. Sheaves with Torlon bearings remain free-turning even under heavy loads and are superior to Delrin bearings, which can get chewed up by abrasives, can change shape under load, and get brittle when exposed to ultra-violet rays.

Bristol Bronze has also just introduced a new, original, bronze alloy that has a much greater tensile strength than conventional 304 stainless steel, for those who need it in high-load applications.

Routine maintenance on bronze blocks consists of simply rinsing them out occasionally to flush away abrasives, such as salt and dirt, and an occasional drop of oil (such as 3-in-1). Teflon spray may also be used, and has the advantage that there is no oil to stain sails or wood and the Teflon doesn't attract dust. Aerosol spray cans of Teflon are available with small plastic tubes that can direct the spray directly into the bearings of the block.

As nearly perfect as bronze blocks are, there is one caveat: they shouldn't be used in direct contact with aluminum due to their relationships on the galvanic table.

Stainless steel blocks

Stainless steel blocks have, for decades, been the blocks of choice for most sailors and are nearly the exclusive block material in most recreational boating catalogs. Most of these blocks are made by stamping out the pattern from stainless steel sheet metal. Stainless steel has many advantages. It is strong, easily available, and reasonably good for direct attachment to aluminum. However the name "stainless" may be a misnomer. Stainless steel is made from iron, and iron rusts. It is also subject to crevice corrosion, that is, wherever there is a hairline crevice or crack, or when the stainless steel is deprived of oxygen, rust will form (the rust we find on our topsides or sails is an example). Crevice corrosion occurs when stainless steel is deprived of the one thing that makes it stainless—oxygen. Stainless steel is also subject to failure when welded. This failure is called weld-decay, carbide-precipitation, or weld-migration, and the insidious condition usually progresses with little indication of a problem, until there is a sudden failure, without warning, of that part.

Why do some of those stainless steel fittings that we bought 25 years ago still look bright and shiny while the ones we bought last year are showing rust stains? A couple of decades ago stainless steel was treated with a procedure called passivation. In this process the stainless steel was immersed in an acid bath and the iron on the surface was eliminated, leaving bright and shiny nickel and chrome. In recent years, however, EPA rules on the disposal of these acid baths have made the process economically prohibitive—except for parts being made for NASA or for the medical industry.

Most stainless steel blocks use metal for the high-load components and plastic for the block cheeks. These plastic cheeks only serve to keep the line running smoothly on the sheave. Although some small, low-load stainless steel blocks have sheaves that rotate directly on the axle, most mid-range and big boat blocks now use roller bearings made of modern, high-tech materials such as Delrin or Torlon. The one small problem with these miracle plastics is that if heavy loads are left on the blocks for extended periods of time the bearings can temporarily deform slightly. Normally the bearings will return to their proper shape after being rotated, but an initial resistance to rolling may be felt. Although big boat block bearings are generally resistant to this deformation, as a rule of thumb it is not advisable to leave strains on any hardware when the boat is not being used.

Most manufacturers of stainless steel blocks who use Delrin or Torlon roller bearings recommend that no oil products be used to lubricate the bearings, since this can attract dirt and cause abrasion. They suggest periodical flushing of the bearings with water, or detergent and water, to remove the salt and dirt. Then a dry lubricant, such as a silicone or Teflon spray, or a proprietary product, such as Harken's "McLube," may be used.

Often as stainless steel blocks age and are exposed to the sun, their black plastic cheeks begin to turn a gray color. This doesn't affect their strength, and the discoloration may be removed with a fine abrasive. If an abrasive is used for cosmetic purposes, be sure to thoroughly flush out the bearings after working on the block.

Wooden blocks

Many traditionally-rigged or older sailboats, as well as even some newer boats, find wooden blocks (or, to be more accurate, wooden-cheek blocks) to be practical on board. Although these blocks may appear to be old and out of date, they actually incorporate several advantages over many of their modern counterparts. Wooden blocks are not only beautiful and strong, but they are designed to be easily disassembled in a matter of minutes for cleaning, lubricating or part-changing. This can be an advantage over some of the more modern blocks, which can't be taken apart at all. Thus, a properly maintained wooden block can provide many decades of service. From the standpoint of preventive maintenance and ease of operation, wooden blocks should be serviced every few years. After wooden blocks have seen several years of use, bring them home at the end of the season, when the boat is decommissioned. Then you can "play boat" during the winter months in the warmth of the workshop, garage, or at the kitchen table.

The first step in disassembling a wooden block is to remove the two metal side plates that cover the ends of the axle. These side plates are usually made of bronze and frequently embossed with the name of the manufacturer. Normally, each plate is held in place with two screws. Sometimes, on more inexpensive or older blocks, nails are used. If the cover plate is fastened with nails, discard them at the first overhaul and replace them with screws. This will make your next maintenance job much easier. Once the screws or nails have been removed, most axle covers can be easily pried off, exposing the ends of the axle. Sometimes the end plates will be recessed into the wooden cheek of the block. The easiest way to remove these is to pry them loose with an ice pick inserted into one of the end-plate screw holes. Infrequently, on some wooden blocks, you may find axle covers that don't want to come off. This probably means that the covers are threaded onto the end of the axle shaft and will have to be unscrewed to be removed. Usually they can be unscrewed using a nail or ice-pick in one of the screw holes, but for stubborn ones a "key," similar to a deck-plate key, might have to be fabricated (two nails driven through a small piece of wood usually does the job).

With the side plates removed, you can now push out the axle. The axle is supported by a metal strap that runs down close to the sheave on the inside of the wooden cheeks. These metal straps take all of the load on the block. The wooden cheeks simply keep the line from running off the sheave. These support straps used to be made from iron, steel, or bronze, but in most of today's wooden blocks they are stainless steel. The axle shaft is not supposed to rotate inside the support straps, since rotation will cause wear on both the axle and the support straps. To ensure that the axle doesn't rotate there will sometimes be a key-pin inserted in one end of the axle shaft.

Now, using a hammer and a screwdriver, the axle can be tapped out. Most axles can be removed from either side, but axles with a key-pin on one end, obviously, can only be driven out from the opposite side.

With the axle removed, the sheave is free to be pushed out of the block. Sheaves can be made from various materials: wood, steel, bronze, and phenolic laminates such as Micarta or from Delrin. Although bronze is probably the most long-lasting and maintenance-free, Micarta and Delrin are close seconds and offer the advantage of less weight aloft. If the sheave is bronze it will usually have stainless steel or bronze roller bearings. Micarta sheaves generally rotate on an oil-impregnated "oilite" bushing and Delrin sheaves

37

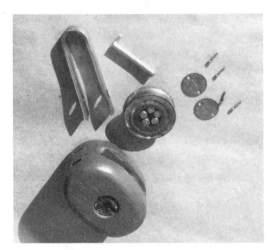

A disassembled wood block

frequently rotate directly on the axle, or on bronze, Delrin or Torlon bearings.

Most heavy duty, top-of-the-line wooden blocks have roller bearings. Usually roller bearings are locked captive into a race inside the sheave—but not always. So, when disassembling any block for the first time it's a good idea to do this inside a dishpan—and not on deck. We've all learned that when we drop something while on deck it has the habit of taking that one bounce, then, as if in slow motion, it neatly hops over the side.

Before re-lubricating the parts, they should first be cleaned of old lubricant. The problem with oil or grease is that it attracts dirt, which can cause wear. For blocks that have been lubricated with oil or grease, the old petroleum can be dissolved by soaking them in kerosene ("paraffin" in Britain) for an hour or two, or overnight. This will usually eliminate the old lubricant. If anything remains, then scrubbing with an old toothbrush does the job.

Once they are clean, it's time to re-lubricate the bearings. Most block manufacturers today recommend lubricating blocks with a dry lubricant, such as generic products like a dry Teflon spray. There are also specialty dry lubricants specifically designed for this purpose. If you insist on a petroleum lubricant, manufacturers suggest that just a single drop of 3-in-1 oil is an alternative.

With the end plates, axle and sheave removed from the wooden shell, you can now slide out the strap that carries the block's load, leaving only the wood shell of the block. This is the perfect time to sand, varnish or oil the wood, without the worry of sawdust getting into the workings of the block. When completely finished, the block can be reassembled, good as new.

So, regardless of the type of block you use, with just a little periodic TLC you can keep your running rigging rolling smoothly and save the expense of re-rigging. It also pays off by making it easier to hoist sail and handle sheets.

Ropes

Rope is the product of cordage manufacturers, but, with a few exceptions, when ropes of less than 1-inch diameter are used aboard a sailboat for a specific function, they become lines. (The etymology of the word *line* is from the Latin, *linea*, which means thread). Until relatively recently the dimension given for a rope was its circumference—thus, a 3-inch hawser was one of 3 inches in circumference, or a little less than 1-inch in diameter. Now, rope dimension is usually given as the diameter.

Until the middle of the 1900s there was a very limited choice of rope (or line, if you wish) from which the sailor could choose—hemp, sisal, and cotton. Now, many synthetic lines have come on the market and, surprisingly, they are now often cheaper than their natural fiber counterparts.

The manufacturing of three-strand rope has not appreciably changed, however. It starts with a small *fiber*. Several of these fibers are twisted into a *thread*. These *threads*, in turn, are twisted into *yarns*, and then the yarns are twisted into *strands*. Finally, three of these strands are twisted into a "three-strand laid rope," the traditional form of rope that was first made from natural fibers. It is common practice that three-strand rope has a right hand twist, although a left hand twist rope is sometimes encountered. With three strand twisted and laid rope there is considerable stretch, however, since the three twisted strands tend to straighten out under tension. The construction of the more modern braided rope reduces this stretching tendency.

Braided rope has a braided outside sheath and an inner core, which can be one of several varieties:

Parallel core is a braided cover enclosing a core whose bundle of fibers and threads are oriented parallel to the line's axis.

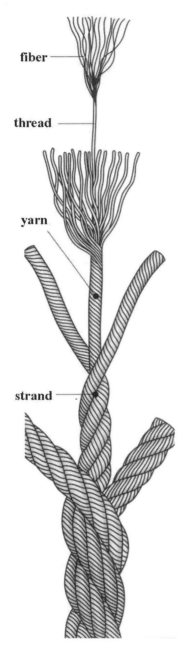

fiber

thread

yarn

strand

Laid rope,
courtesy of Ted Tollefson

Double braided is a braided cover over a braided core of the same material.

Core-loaded double braid is a braided cover over a braided low-stretch core of a different material.

There are three basic man-made fibers that have been used by sailors for decades: nylon, polyester (usually called Dacron in the United States and Terylene in Britain), and polypropylene. Of these three basic synthetic ropes, nylon is the strongest, with polyester a close second, and finally polypropylene.

Best choice

Since nylon has high strength, excellent abrasion resistance, and great elasticity, it is the best choice for use where there will be shock loads, such as for dock lines and anchor lines. But those same attributes make it completely unsuited for use as running rigging—such as halyards—where stretch would be a detriment.

Polyester, on the other hand, provides almost as much strength as nylon, but with little stretch. When purchased "pre-stretched," its elongation under load is even less. It also has good abrasion resistance. This makes it the all-around choice for most other applications on board.

Polypropylene has the lowest strength of the three. It is relatively cheap, and has the advantage of being lighter than water, so it floats. This makes it the line of choice for dinghy painters, reducing the possibility of its sinking and fouling the propeller. Polypropylene, though, is much more

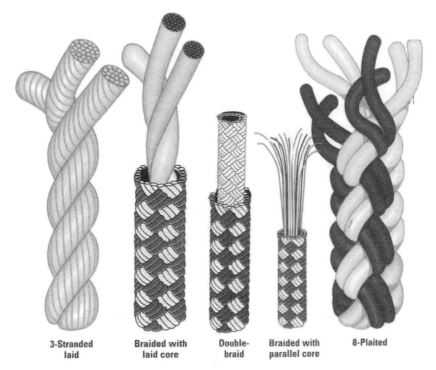

| 3-Stranded laid | Braided with laid core | Double-braid | Braided with parallel core | 8-Plaited |

Laid, braided and plaited rope, *courtesy of Ted Tollefson*

susceptible to ultra-violet deterioration, and is also subject to melting when cornering through a chock under high tension.

Beyond these three basic fiber groups are a plethora of more expensive options, as well as their associated high-tech terminology. Some of these new terms are:

High Modulus, which basically means low-stretch. Most of the high modulus lines are very slippery and, when tied with the knots that we know well, are prone to failure. Although a bowline in a nylon or polyester line decreases the strength of that line by about 40%, in a high-modulus line the strength is reduced by an astounding 70% or more. For this reason knots should be avoided in high modulus lines, in favor of splices.

LCP (liquid crystal polymer), such as Vectran, is one of the latest rope-making fibers. These thermoplastics are very strong and abrasion resistant, but have low UV resistance.

HMWPE (high molecular weight polyethylene) includes ropes such as Spectra, Amsteel, and Dyneema. Despite its high strength, HMWPE is so lightweight that it floats. Pound for pound it has 10 times the strength of steel and is three times stronger than polyester. It is also low stretch (stretching takes place during the manufacturing process). It has good abrasion- and UV-resistance, but it is high priced and is very slippery.

Aramids are in the nylon family and are marketed under the names Kevlar, Technora, and Twaron. Although they are high strength with relatively low stretch, they have poor UV- and abrasion-resistance, especially when subjected to sharp bends under load.

Line care

There are general rules that apply to all types of lines to help extend their life:

During the boating season hose off lines with fresh water to wash away dirt and salt crystals, and at the end of the season soak the lines in warm soapy water, then rinse them off and hang them up to dry.

Remove all the lines possible from your boat during the off season, especially those with a low UV tolerance. This will extend their life considerably.

Belaying Pins

We've all seen belaying pins in vintage pirate movies or on our visits to the Tall Ships, but on today's modern sailboats? Of course not. They're out of style, impractical, archaic—and I love them!

The belaying pins of yesteryear were made of hardwood, usually locust, and sometimes bronze, iron, or brass. They were used to secure and store lines, particularly the running rigging. Securing a line to a belaying pin is the same as to a cleat. To provide increased friction to control a line, the line is "belayed." To belay a line is to secure it by taking a single round turn and one or more S-turns around the cleat or belaying pin. When a single hitch or slip-hitch is added to the belayed turns, the line is "made fast." Thus, to belay a line is not the same as to make fast a line. One of the big advantages of belaying pins over cleats is the speed and ease with which a line that is belayed, or made fast, can be released. When the belaying pin is pulled, the line falls to the deck in an untangled flaked-out pattern, ready to run freely.

The old sailing ships frequently set their belaying pins in holes in the pinrail, which was fixed inside the bulwarks or incorporated as part of the bulwark or main rail. Short pinrails, fastened to the standing rigging are called pin racks, and around the mast on deck, pin racks of rectangular or U shape, called fiferails, are used to make fast and store halyards. A variation of the fiferail is used on modern sailboats, where the pulpit is combined with a small pin rack. A spider-band was sometimes fitted around a wooden mast a little above deck level, with holes for the belaying pins. This was sometimes called a "spider hoop" or "spider iron." Stanchion-mounted pin racks are used on more modern boats for storing coils of line, and are both decorative and utilitarian.

For the do-it-yourselfer, belaying pins can be turned out on the most basic of lathes from brass, bronze, or scrap hardwood—but remember, those metal ones don't float! With today's teak prices, it's nice to know that those teak scraps can be turned into beautiful belaying pins for on-board use, or even for home decoration.

Our schooner is rigged in the old Grand Banks manner, with no sheet winches. To attain mechanical advantage, multiple-part block and tackle is used for each of the sheets. This presents the problem of long coils of line ending up in the cockpit due to the 4:1 block ratio. This would be a colossal spaghetti pot if it weren't for the belaying pin racks we've installed, not for belaying as such, but rather as an attractive and practical rack for keeping our sheets out from underfoot.

I built our schooner, DELPHINUS, from a bare fiberglass hull. The Ted Brewer design was a scaled down replica of the old New England fishing schooners, and I tried to maintain the theme by incorporating belaying pin racks on the shrouds of the foremast and mainmast, on the boom-gallows stanchions, and at the forward end of the cockpit. Although I had never used belaying pins before, I thought that they belonged on board a schooner. Now I can't imagine sailing without them. They add that needed touch of character, as well as being completely useful—and don't forget, they're good for dispatching that fish you caught on the lure trailing astern—or for fighting off pirates.

Belaying pins on DELPHINUS

44

Bowsprits, Bumpkins, and Belaying Pins

If you remember when all sailboats had wood spars, manila lines, galvanized fittings, and cotton sails, chances are you have problems with your waistline, your hairline and the number of teeth you can call your own. Those of us who fit this category have a special feeling for those sailboats of our youth, but those fond memories don't include the maintenance involved in boats of that period.

When people see our schooner, DELPHINUS, sail by, they see a boat from the turn of the century, a schooner rig with bowsprit, figurehead, bumpkin, belaying pins, wooden blocks, bronze portholes, lazyjacks, and a graceful sheer. Yet it's only 28 years old, with fiberglass hull, aluminum spars, and modern conveniences throughout—a modern version of a small Down East schooner of the last century. It's one of the breed sailors call "character boats," befitting of its skipper. Boats such as this are the rediscovery in fiberglass of traditional cruising boats, such as schooners, catboats, Friendship sloops, and other designs from the past. Not only is there warmth about their appealing lines and traditional rigs, but below decks, you may be in a fiberglass boat but you feel like you're in a wooden one.

While the conscious mind is thinking, "It looks dated—probably slow," sneaking into the subconscious are thoughts of coastal trading, the Grand Banks, Tahiti, and the whole mystique of other times, faraway places and nostalgia. But traditional beauty doesn't necessarily mean being impractical.

Bowsprits

Take the bowsprit for example. On our schooner it provides a sailplan longer than the boat's hull. With a lower center of effort, there is less heeling and more sail can be carried. This translates into drive power. When tied up at a mooring buoy in an area with wind, current, and tide changes, a bull rope from the tip of the bowsprit can prevent the hull from striking the mooring buoy. This bull rope consists of an extra line from the ring of the buoy to the tip of the bowsprit, with just enough tension to keep the mooring buoy away from the bow.

Bowsprits traditionally found homes on cruising boats, but then, for several decades, they were abandoned. In the last few years a resurgence in bowsprits has occurred with the reproduction of old designs as well as in the racing classes that allow them. When using a bowsprit, more of the headsail is free from interference with the main, and in fresh wind conditions, the more forward center of effort reduces weather helm and pressure on the rudder.

In many of these racing boats, the bowsprit is made retractable, either into the hull or along the deck, and unguyed carbon-fiber bowsprits are now emerging on the scene.

The bowsprit and leaping dolphin figurehead
aboard our schooner, DELPHINUS

Our solid teak bowsprit provides a perfect platform to sit and watch the bow wave or the dolphins, and without a bowsprit, where would we put the figurehead?

Figureheads

A millennium before Christ, the Egyptians carved the heads of deities on the bows of their ships, and the Romans, Greeks, and Phoenicians carried on this tradition, dedicating their ships to their gods and goddesses in the hope of ensuring safe voyages. The dragon ships of the Vikings were adorned with menacing carved-oak, snarling dragon heads, intended to terrify the raiders' victims and also guard against evil spirits at sea. The power of figureheads was considered so great that at one time Iceland insisted that foreign ships remove them before entering her waters.

Captain Bligh reported that the Tahitians were fascinated with the figurehead on the HMS BOUNTY. He described it as "a pretty figure of a woman in a riding habit," who was lifting her skirts over the seas with her right hand as she looked ahead of the ship. This painted likeness was the first representation of an English woman the Tahitians had ever seen. Bligh wrote: ". . . and they kept gazing at it for hours."

Although a century or two ago, figureheads became merely ornamental, many American commercial, and even naval ships, were still sent to sea with elaborate carvings at their bows. The frigate CONSTITUTION was launched in 1797, adorned with a bust of Hercules. But Hercules was not up to the foray with the Barbary Coast pirates at Tripoli, where the figurehead was destroyed.

Our schooner, DELPHINUS, is named for the constellation of the dolphin, and sports a carved teak figurehead of a leaping dolphin beneath her bowsprit. It serves not only as a decorative appendage, but also as a bowsprit brace. It's a great hit both on the water and at dock side, and seems to have a special attraction for children.

As enlightened sailors, we know our figurehead is purely decorative— and yet, sometimes there's the feeling of a presence at our bow, guiding us through foggy and unfamiliar waters.

Belaying pins

Belaying pins are used to provide increased friction to control a line by taking a single round-turn and one or more S turns around the pin. This is to belay the line. When a single hitch or slip-hitch is added to the belayed turns, the line is made fast.

The bumpkin

And, oh yes, let's not forget the bumpkin (sometimes called boomkin or bumkin). We have one on our schooner also, but how many modern-day sailors have heard that term? The bumpkin is a short boom, frequently V-shaped, extending out from the stern, to which the backstay or mizzen sheet block is attached. When used for the backstay, along with an associated bumpkin stay, it allows a longer mainsail boom and frequently eliminates the need for running backstays. For the ketch or yawl it provides a more practical lead-angle for the mizzen sheet. On our schooner the mainsail extends all the way to the stern of the boat, with the bumpkin keeping the permanent backstay well out of the way.

For years we looked for a retirement boat that would fill our specs till we happened to stumble across our little schooner design from the board of Ted Brewer. It meets our needs completely, and seems appropriate for our vintage years. When we sail by, with everything up, people turn to watch or take pictures. And with that old, gray-haired, bearded character at the wheel, they probably think it's an apparition from the past. After all, how often do you see a small schooner with bowsprit, wooden blocks, figurehead, belaying pins, and a boomkin?

Electronics

GPS, DGPS, and WAAS

The early days

Today there are about 2,700 man-made satellites circling the Earth, but our satellite age had very humble beginnings. Twelve years after the end of World War II, in October 1957, the first man-made satellite was thrust into orbit around the Earth. The USSR's tiny *Sputnik* had beaten the United States into space—or so the world believed. Actually the US was also prepared to launch a satellite, but held off for political reasons.

Till that time, any foreign aircraft flying over a country had to have permission to use that country's airspace, and the same still holds true today; but what about a satellite? If the US allowed the USSR to launch a satellite and have it fly over countries all over the world, including the United States, without protest, then a new international law would be established—and the US was sure that with its technology, a US satellite could be used for spying on the USSR. Remember, this was at the height of the Cold War. Once Sputnik established the precedent with no protests, the US launched their own satellite.

The US, in an effort to learn as much about Sputnik as possible, monitored the beeping signal it transmitted, and was able to determine its location through the Doppler effect. This was the genesis of using man-made satellites to determine navigational information. But it wasn't till the 1970s that the satellite navigation system, as we now know it, began to take shape.

Because of limited booster-rocket technology, the early satellites had to have a low-weight payload, and the limited power of the booster rockets could not put the satellite into a very high orbit. In fact the early satellites were just on the outer edge of the Earth's atmosphere. This is termed a Low Earth Orbit (LEO). For all satellites, both man-made and natural, their height above the Earth determines their orbital (angular) speed. The early LEO satellites had Earth orbits of two hours or less. Sputnik, at a height of 560 miles, orbited the Earth every 96 minutes. By contrast, we have a satellite that's over ¼-million miles away from the Earth and takes 28 days to complete an orbit—it's our Moon.

As booster rockets increased in size, larger satellites could be launched into higher orbits. Finally, a satellite was put into an orbit 22,240 miles (35,786 km) above the equator, in an orbit rotating in the same direction as the rotation of the Earth. This height was a magical number.

In 1945, when man-made satellites were still considered a fantasy, science-fiction writer Arthur C. Clarke proposed that if a satellite could be put into orbit above the equator at a height of 22,240 miles above the surface of the Earth, its angular orbital speed would be the same as that of the Earth, and it would appear to be motionless in the sky. This type of

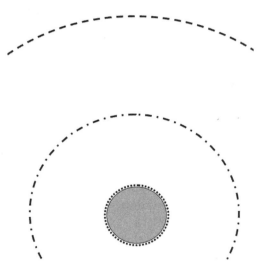

A comparison of the orbital heights of geostationary satellites, shown in a dashed line (22,240 m, 35,786 km), and a Low Earth Orbital band, shown in a dotted line, which includes the Space Shuttle (100–520 nm, 185–1,000 km), the International Space Station (220 m, 360 km), the Hubble Telescope (325 nm, 600 km), as well as Search and Rescue satellites and a host of other Low Earth Orbit (LEO) services, and the intermediate GPS Constellation orbit, shown in a dot-dash line.

satellite is now called a geostationary satellite. Satellites with an orbital time of 24 hours are termed geosynchronous, but these are not necessarily geostationary, such as when their orbits are canted to the equator and elliptical. (A geostationary satellite is also a geosynchronous satellite, but the reverse is not necessarily true). In the early 1960s communications satellites were launched into just such an orbit. They became the first of many.

Today's GPS system

The NAVSTAR Global Positioning System (GPS) became fully operational in 1995. GPS is a satellite navigation system that was designed for and is operated by the US military, but it is now used by millions of civilians worldwide. The basic space segment of this system, known as the GPS Operational Constellation, consists of a minimum of 24 satellites that orbit the Earth twice a day. There are often more than 24 in space, as new ones are placed in orbit to replace those whose on-board fuel is becoming exhausted.

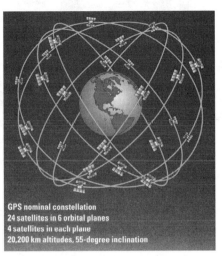

GPS nominal constellation
24 satellites in 6 orbital planes
4 satellites in each plane
20,200 km altitudes, 55-degree inclination

GPS nominal constellation,
courtesy of Ted Tollefson

There are six separate satellite orbits, or orbital planes, with a minimum of four satellites traveling in each of these orbital planes. These orbits are spaced around the equator 60 degrees apart, and their orbital planes are canted about 55 degrees to the equatorial plane.

This GPS constellation configuration provides the user at any point on earth with five or more visible satellites at any time. With access to just three satellites, a two-dimensional fix (latitude and longitude) can be determined, and with four satellites, GPS receivers can compute a location in three dimensions. This makes the GPS navigation system ideal for aircraft, as well as for boats, ground transportation, and hikers. Each GPS satellite contains an atomic clock, and by measuring the time interval between the transmission and reception of a satellite signal, a spherical line-of-position is created around each satellite. The intersection of these spherical lines-of-position determines your location.

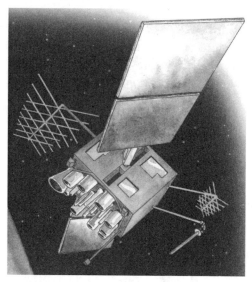

GPS satellite,
courtesy of Ted Tollefson

The GPS satellites transmit in the microwave spectrum. At these frequencies the wavelength is very short and the receiving antenna can consequently be very small. One of the problems with this frequency is that it does not easily pass through things like house roofs, cabin tops, or people (if you're holding a hand-held GPS at waist-height, the receiver has difficulty acquiring a satellite from the other side of your body).

Error corrections

When initially put into service, the GPS system was so accurate, that the Department of Defense deliberately introduced an error into the civilian GPS system to prevent its use by terrorists. However this error, *Selective Availability* (SA), caused a potential hazard to users. If a boat were coming through a narrow inlet in a fog, the error that was introduced by Selective Availability, possibly up to 300 feet or more, could put the boat on the rocks. So the U.S. Coast Guard, at a cost of millions of dollars, established low-frequency AM ground stations along the coast. Accessing the data from one of these Coast Guard stations would take out the error introduced by the Department of Defense. This system, *Differential GPS* (DGPS), requires a separate antenna system and receiver, which is frequently more expensive than the GPS receiver itself. Finally, in May 2000, the Selective Availability error was discontinued, and overnight GPS users worldwide had a dramatically more accurate system.

However there were still potential errors in the system—such as clock errors, ionosheric and troposheric delays as the signal travels from the satellites to earth, earth reflections, satellite orbital drifts, and control errors. The DGPS ground stations could reduce most of these errors. But those stations, which required the separate receiver and antenna, had limited range and, since they were AM transmitters, were subject to noise and fading. Geostationary satellites, operating in the same frequency band as the GPS satellites, were put in orbit, and those new stationary satellites provided corrections that could be received directly on a GPS antenna without the need of a separate receiver and antenna system. This improved correction system is known as the Wide Area Augmentation System (WAAS).

Irregularities

Now, if you imagine that these 24 GPS satellites are orbiting around a sphere in space, the Earth, you are wrong. In 300 B.C. the Greeks established that the Earth was a sphere, but it's not a sphere. Due to its rotation, it bulges out at the equator and is flattened at the poles. Now if the GPS receiver believed that the Earth is a sphere, if you were sailing near the equator, and took an altitude measurement from your GPS, it would tell you that you were 25 miles high, since you are on top of the equatorial bulge. Not only altitude is affected, since this bulge also stretches the lines of latitude and longitude.

The shape of the Earth is actually more like what is known in solid geometry as an ellipsoid. Ellipsoids come in all types of mathematical shapes, and the first ellipsoid to represent the Earth was promulgated in 1866, and was known as the Clarke Ellipsoid.

By the 20th century we knew that the Clarke Ellipsoid was not that accurate, and in North America, we developed the North American Datum Ellipsoid of 1927 (NAD-27). Although this ellipsoid was fairly accurate for North America, it wasn't for the rest of the world and the World Geodetic Survey developed a new mathematical model in 1966. It was called the World Geodetic Survey Ellipsoid of 1966, or WGS-66. The mathematical models continued to be refined, with WGS-72 following, till, finally, WGS-84 was developed. In North America a new ellipsoid was also proposed, the NAD-83. The NAD-83 and the WGS-84 are, for all practical purposes, identical.

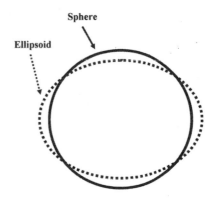

But any specific location on the face of the Earth can be defined by different latitudes and longitudes, depending on the *Chart Datum* or *Map Datum* used to make the measurement. And around the world there are hundreds of different datums and charts whose latitude and longitude lines do not coincide with WGS-84 / NAD-83. Your GPS receiver can be programmed for many different Chart Datums, but nearly all GPS receivers now sold have a default that puts them on the WGS-84 / NAD-83 ellipsoid model.

It is very important that the latitude and longitude lines on the chart you are using (the *Chart Datum* or *Map Datum*) make use of the same measuring system as your GPS receiver. Fortunately all US charts now use latitude and longitude lines based on the WGS-84 / NAD-83 ellipsoid, but other charts outside of the US may be using a different model. If so, that *Chart Datum* model is generally printed on the chart. When using that chart and navigating with GPS, your GPS should be reset for that specific *datum*. Most modern GPS receivers have a hundred or more different worldwide *Chart Datums* available. These can be accessed and used to replace the default *Chart Datum* by entering the *Menu*, *System*, and *Units* tabs.

The geoid

Due to differences in gravity at various points on the Earth's surface, that surface is not a smooth mathematical ellipsoid. It has depressions and bulges and the actual shape of the Earth is known as a geoid. The geoid is the sea-level surface of the Earth and is considerably smoother than the Earth's physical surface, which has mountains and valleys. This sea-level geoid, however, varies plus and minus about 100 meters (over 328 feet) from the theoretical WGS-84 / NAD-83 ellipsoid. Programming a GPS

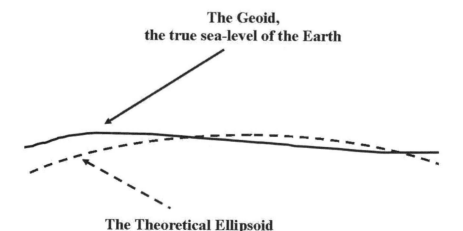

**The Geoid,
the true sea-level of the Earth**

The Theoretical Ellipsoid

receiver for a geoid takes a large amount of memory, since the true shape of the Earth, the geoid, doesn't follow any simple mathematical formula.

So if you have an older, inexpensive GPS, and you look at your altitude when sitting in your boat off the coast of New Jersey, for example, you'll see that your elevation is about 70 feet above sea level. But if you have a relatively modern, expensive GPS receiver, with the geoid irregularities entered into its memory, it compensates for the fact that this section of the East Coast is on one of the Earth's geoidal bulges and indicates that you are at sea level.

The GPS and relativity

In the early 1900s, Albert Einstein challenged our Newtonian concepts about time and space. In today's world we imagine that his theory of relativity doesn't affect our lives—yet every time we get a GPS fix, we are making use of his concepts, since the GPS is a measurement of time and space.

In his special theory of relativity, Einstein postulated that as velocity increases, time slows down. In 1972 this was proven in the most basic of ways when atomic clocks were put aboard military jets and sent on a high-velocity trip around the world. When they were returned to Earth, they had slowed down compared with identical terrestrial atomic clocks. Because of their velocity, time had been slower during their flight by just the amount that Albert Einstein had predicted.

Every GPS satellite has atomic clocks on board, and since these satellites are traveling at a velocity of about 2.5 miles per second, time is slower, and the atomic clocks on board are no longer in sync with the ones on Earth—yet this in-sync requirement is fundamental to the GPS measurement process.

Although time aboard these satellites only loses about 7 microseconds a day, the whole GPS system measures time within a few nanoseconds to derive its fix, and 7 microseconds are 7,000 nanoseconds.

Einstein's general theory of relativity postulates that as gravity decreases, time speeds up. So the atomic clocks run faster in the GPS satellites.

The result of the velocity/time slow-down of time (7 microseconds/day), and the gravity/time speed-up of time (45 microseconds/day), is that the atomic clocks on the satellites gain 38 microseconds/day—38,000 nanoseconds/day.

The results of relativity thus make GPS unusable, unless corrections are made for relativity. To make these corrections, on-board micro-computers take the fast atomic clock time, and through relativistic algorithms (the

Kalman filter algorithm and the Gaussian error algorithm), the atomic clock time on the satellite is mathematically modified to account for relativity, so that the signal broadcast is in sync with the clocks on Earth.

GPS vulnerability

There's no doubt that GPS is a fantastic navigational tool, but I'm suggesting that you don't throw away your Loran receiver yet. Loran and GPS offer complimentary technologies, and are not prone to the same modes of failure—which makes them ideal backups for each other. Whereas GPS is a satellite system that receives very small amounts of radio-frequency power from orbiting satellites and which operates at extremely high frequency, Loran is a land-based system that sends out a very high powered radio wave and operates on an extremely low frequency. The very fact that GPS operates on an unbelievably small amount of received power makes it very susceptible to jammers or hackers—and in the present world atmosphere this becomes more and more of a probability every day. For anyone with a good knowledge of electronics, and about a hundred dollars, the weak GPS signals received from orbiting satellites can be easily disrupted over a wide area. Conversely, it would take a huge antenna array and very large and high powered equipment to create a similar problem for Loran.

Several years ago in the U.S. there was a move to phase out Loran, since GPS was so much more accurate and practical—but this was in the days before global terrorism. Most other countries operating their own Loran systems have never favored the idea of making a complete changeover to GPS, and have actually been increasing their Loran coverage.

Suddenly, a few years ago, nations around the world were alerted to the vulnerability of the GPS system when, at the 1997 Moscow Air Show, a jammer disabled the GPS signals over a 150 mile radius. The implications from that awakening created a new policy in the US, one that recognizes that a backup system, Loran, should remain in place.

On occasion, the US Federal Government conducts GPS interference tests, exercises and training activities that involve jamming GPS receivers. These events go through a lengthy coordination process involving the Federal Aviation Administration (FAA), the US Coast Guard (USCG), the Department of Defense (DoD) and other government agencies. A list of the times and locations of these jamming tests is available on the USCG's Navigation website.

Other global positioning systems

Nearly all of the rest of the world also uses the U.S. GPS system for navigation. But since this system was developed, and is controlled, by the U.S. military, it is looked on with suspicion outside this country. In addition, the geostationary WAAS satellites that were launched by the United States have a footprint that provides only for limited correctional coverage. To solve this problem, Asia has launched a separate WAAS-type satellite, the MSAS. European countries are developing their own global positioning systems patterned after the U.S. GPS system. Currently there are two proposed systems, the Russian GLONASS (Global Navigation Satellite System), and the Galileo Positioning System which, so that it is not abbreviated the same as the U.S. GPS system, is simply called Galileo. Both systems are scheduled to be operational by 2010.

Communication protocol

As improvements continue, consumer prices for GPS receivers keep dropping, while accuracy, operational simplicity, and extra features are expanding. GPS receivers have the ability to communicate with other electronic equipment on board, such as an EPIRB, electronic chart plotter, autopilot, VHF-FM radio, radar, etc. But in order to carry on their conversation, they must be talking the same language. The standard protocol for years has been the "NMEA 0183." Newer units now use the "NMEA 2000" protocol, which contains the standard of a serial-data network to interconnect marine electronics designed for this protocol. Equipment designed for this standard has the ability to share data, including commands and status. Although the interconnection of equipment has traditionally been by wire, newer units interconnect using wireless technology. Most chart plotters combine the GPS location overlaid on an electronic chart. These units have a very small battery drain, and provide today's sailor with navigational capabilities undreamed of a few decades ago. In addition, an EPIRB with an integral GPS gives Search and Rescue the exact location of the distress signal immediately, eliminating the time that formerly was necessary to compute the location through Doppler.

Loran

Loran-C provides navigation, location, and timing services for both civil and military air, land, and marine users. The LORAN-C system serves the 48 continental states, their coastal areas, and parts of Alaska. For most recreational boaters, however, a Loran receiver is a thing of the past, replaced by the more accurate Global Positioning System (GPS), which has a smaller antenna, is more accurate, and can be easily interfaced with a large selection of chart plotters or combined electronic gear (Multi-Functional Displays, MFDs).

Electronic navigation history

GPS and Loran-C are the two primary electronic navigation systems used by boaters today. Loran (an acronym for Long RAnge Navigation) is a hyperbolic navigation system, so named because the lines of position are hyperbolas. Several other hyperbolic navigation systems have also been developed over the years: England's privately-owned Decca; Germany's Consol; and the US Navy's Omega. One of the first Loran systems, Loran-A, was developed for the US Navy and operated at a frequency of 1.9 MHz. It had a limited range of 450-800 miles, with an accuracy within 1.5-7 miles—similar to the accuracy of celestial navigation using a sextant.

Today's Loran-C

In 1957 a greatly improved and much more complex Loran system, with longer range and more accuracy, became operational. It was designated as Loran-C, our present system. Loran-C operates at a very low frequency, 100 kHz, but with very high power. This low frequency and high power makes signal reception beyond 1,000 miles possible, and the radio waves even penetrate into surface waters, allowing their use by submarines. The land-based transmitters consist of a *master* station and up to four *slave*, or *secondary* stations. Each group of the master and its associated slave stations is called a *chain*. In a chain, the master station is designated by the letter M, and the slave stations are designated W, X, Y, and Z.

The accurately-synchronized signals from these stations are controlled by atomic clocks, and the Time-Difference (TD) between the reception of signals from the master and the slaves creates the hyperbolic lines of position. These lines of position are overprinted onto many charts and, as in all navigation systems, the intersection of two or more of these lines of position determines the fix.

Loran was initially developed as a navigational tool for US coastal waters, but was expanded to provide complete coverage of the continental United States and Alaskan coast.

The early Loran receivers were only used aboard naval vessels. They had 52 operational controls, weighed over 100 pounds, and required a skilled operator. As computer technology progressed, Loran sizes and operational complications were reduced, and receivers became practical

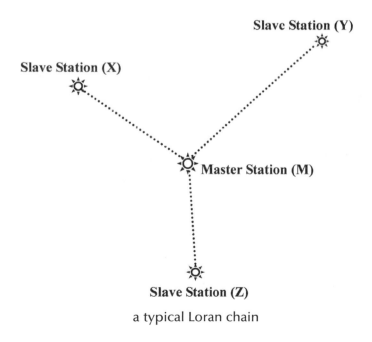

a typical Loran chain

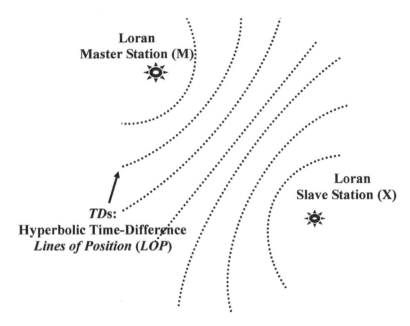

**Loran
Master Station (M)**

TDs:
Hyperbolic Time-Difference
Lines of Position (LOP)

**Loran
Slave Station (X)**

The hyperbolic lines of position between
the *Master* station (M) and a *Slave (X)*

aboard recreational craft. Finally, complicated algorithms, programmed into the receiver's computer, were able to transpose the hyperbolic lines of position into latitude and longitude. This worked well enough in the open ocean, but one of the characteristics of Loran's hyperbolic lines of position is that they become distorted when crossing over land masses, so that, in many cases, plotting the TD lines on the chart provides a better fix than having the receiver's computer calculate a theoretical one. Even though the accuracy of Loran does not match that of GPS, its repeatability, that is, the ability to return to exactly the same spot again and again, is excellent. For this reason many fishermen and wreck-divers still use their library of Loran-C Time Difference waypoints to return to their favorite locations.

Loran antennas for recreational boats usually consist of a 4- or 8-foot vertical whip, which is screwed into an "antenna-coupler." The coupler is a vital part of the antenna system. Since the Loran wavelength is extremely long (over a mile) and the antenna is very short by comparison, the antenna coupler matches the extremely long wavelength of Loran and the comparatively short receiving antenna so that the signals can be used efficiently by the receiver. Due to the very low frequency of the Loran signal, the height of this antenna is relatively unimportant.

New Loran receivers are hard to come by and can only be purchased by special order through some marine electronics distributors. Furuno makes one Loran model, which can be ordered through some distributors, including the New Jersey-based Consumers Marine Electronics.

For many boaters, having a Loran receiver on board provides an excellent back-up navigational system. The need of having a reliable backup system on board was dramatically illustrated on Sunday, July 17, 2004, when suddenly all the Icom WP360 chart plotters suddenly crashed simultaneously. It took a month before the problem was solved. All of these units then had to be returned for an upgrade, so that boaters with this particular chart plotter, and no backup system other than a compass, were required to go back to basics.

The U.S. Government will continue to operate Loran-C system in the short term. It will give users reasonable notice if it concludes that Loran-C is not needed or is not cost effective, so that users will have the opportunity to transition to alternative navigation systems. In the meantime Loran-C will continue to provide a supplemental means of navigation.

So, if you've been thinking about removing your old Loran receiver from your console to make room for newer, high-tech equipment, it might be a good idea to reconsider.

VHF-FM

Except for world cruisers, the primary radio communications for small craft is the VHF-FM Marine-Band radio, known as a short range communications system. It is the method of choice for the recreational boater, and a station license from the FCC is no longer required for use within the United States.

VHF stands for Very High Frequency—the band of frequencies between 30 and 300 megahertz (MHz), with wavelengths of 10 to 1 meter, respectively. The marine band, with frequencies between 156-163 MHz, is located in this broad VHF band, which is home to a variety of services, including FM radio, aviation, police, commercial uses such as trucks and taxis, garage door-openers, scientific and medical uses, cordless phones, amateur bands, radio-control, and television channels 2 through 13. Just like the television signals, this marine band is usually described as line-of-sight, so the higher the antenna, the greater the range. (Actually, VHF signals bend slightly, attempting to follow the contour of the earth and, infrequently, when special layers of the ionosphere form a reflective path, they can travel hundreds or thousands of miles).

FM stands for Frequency Modulation—that same type of signal that brings us our FM broadcast stations static-free, as well as the sound on our TV.

Although some people new to boating eschew the marine band radio in favor of their cell phones, this is a bad idea. In an emergency situation, when using the marine band, you can reach the Coast Guard directly, and other boaters nearby can also hear your May Day call and come to your assistance. (May Day is a phonetic way for the English-speaking world to say the French phrase, "Help Me." This term was established in the early part of the last century, before English took over from French as the language of diplomacy and international travel).

The power of a marine band transmitter on a recreational boat is limited to a maximum of 25 watts, that is, the amount of radio-frequency energy that goes into the antenna. It is also required that this power be reduced to 1 watt for short range communications, such as communicating with a bridge operator.

Antennas for the marine band are "vertically polarized." This means that the transmitting antenna element is vertical and, for optimum performance, receiving antennas should also be vertical. (TV antennas, as we have all observed, have horizontal polarization). The gain of a marine band antenna is the measurement of how much of the antenna's transmitting and receiving power is concentrated in a horizontal direction.

For sailboats, a gain of 3 dB is the norm, since any higher gain would concentrate the antenna's transmitting and receiving power into an even narrower horizontal beam, which could be counter-productive when a sailboat is heeled over.

On many marine band radios you will note that a selection can be made between International and USA. This is because on some channels there is a frequency difference between the two. Thus, for routine communications with the Coast Guard, you must tune to Channel 22 with the American frequency (which is easily remembered by the suffix "A"). Hence, the Coast Guard is listed as Channel 22A. If you were to transmit on the International frequency of Channel 22, the Coast Guard wouldn't hear you.

DSC

As originally conceived, the marine band was relatively simple and straightforward. Channels were allocated for distress, safety and calling, the Coast Guard, commercial vessels, recreational boats, ship-to-ship, ship-to-shore, marine operators (who can connect you into the land-line telephone system), and weather.

DSC (Digital Selective Calling) technology is now a part of new marine band radios. Although commercial vessels have had DSC since 1988, it has just recently become available to recreational boaters. With DSC, at the touch of a single button, an automatic May Day call can be transmitted. It includes your Maritime Mobile Service Identification Number (MMSI), which describes your vessel. Also, through an interface with your GPS, your latitude and longitude can also be automatically transmitted, and these DSC-equipped radios can continue transmitting the emergency message, even when the boat has been abandoned. DSC can also be used for making direct phone calls without going through the marine operator, or ship-to-ship calls to other DSC-equipped vessels. The sender and designated receiver for these calls, in contrast to non-DSC calls, are private, and cannot be monitored by every other boat in the vicinity. When a DSC call is originated, the digital alert signal only takes about a half-second. This half-second signal alerts the designated receiver, usually by a buzzer, and the receiver's screen will show the information as to where and how the message will be sent.

A DSC-equipped radio must be registered with the FCC, which can be easily done through BoatUS. The MMSI number of each of these radios is similar to a telephone number, so when making a DSC ship-to-ship call, you must know the MMSI number of the other party.

VHF-FM improvements

Handheld VHF radios have decreased in size and increased in reliability, and many are now submersible, which makes them great for your "abandon ship" bag. Since most sailboats have their 25 watt, fixed-mount VHF in the cabin, a handheld can be a great asset in the cockpit, especially when entering a new marina and receiving directions from the dockmaster, or when talking to a drawbridge operator. But for newer cabin-installed radios there is an alternative: remote microphones that allow channel-selection, entire LCD displays, and a speaker, all in the palm of your hand.

New battery technology has also given longer life to handhelds, with the new nickel-metal hydride (nmh) batteries providing twice as long a time between charging as the old nickel-cadmium rechargeable batteries. But it's still a good idea to keep alkaline batteries in your abandon-ship bag, since they have a shelf-life of over five years, whereas a rechargeable battery can self-discharge in a few months.

Radar

Radar is an acronym for RAdio Detecting And Ranging. A marine radar is used to determine the distances and azimuths of land masses, boats, and buoys by measuring the time between the transmission and return of an electromagnetic microwave signal which has been transmitted and reflected back from the target. In some cases this return signal may also be retransmitted by a transponder on the target, which is triggered by the original signal.

A single rotating, highly directional antenna is used for both transmitting and receiving. The size of the antenna and the frequency of the radar determine the beam width of the transmitted signal, with a very narrow *horizontal beam width* being optimal. This antenna, which rotates through 360 degrees, may be an open array, which presents the most precise display, or a rotating antenna enclosed within a radome, which is preferable for sailboats, since there is no rotating antenna to foul the running rigging. Some of these radomes are as small as 12 inches in diameter—but as the diameter of a radome becomes smaller, the more imprecise is the resultant display.

Since radar frequencies are nearly line-of-sight transmission, the height of the antenna and the height of the target determine the radar's maximum range. The radar transmits very short, yet very high-powered, bursts of microwave energy thousands of times a second. Between the transmitted bursts, the radar is in the receive mode for the reflected signals returning from the target. Due to the high intensity and frequency of this microwave beam, and the fact that the vertical beam width is much greater than the horizontal beam width, it's important not to locate the radar's antenna where the microwave energy will be directed toward any people or animals on board or toward other onboard antennas, such as a GPS.

Radar signals can be attenuated by rain, and to a lesser extent fog. The higher a radar's output power, the greater its ability to produce a usable return signal under these conditions.

Although a radar's power is rated in kilowatts, this only occurs for short periods (usually considerably less than a microsecond) so a modern 12-volt DC LCD radar does not consume much overall power. In addition, these units take up very little physical space, so that even the smallest of boats, for an investment of less than $1000, can now have the security of radar when the fog rolls in.

Operational controls

All modern radars feature automatic and manual controls. Usually, the automatic mode results in the most satisfactory display, but manual adjustments are also available, and can be useful under special circumstances. The range, of course, is operator-selected.

Dual-range displays

As the name implies, a dual-range display allows the simultaneous display of two ranges on a single split screen. Typically this would be a detailed display of the immediate area and, at the same time, a long range display, that allows you to keep a watchful eye on what is approaching in the distance. The operator has the option of selecting the ranges for each display.

Multi-function/single-station displays

In the past few years there have been incredible changes in marine electronics. One of these is the multi-function display (MFD), which can provide, on one screen, two or more of your boat's navigational electronics, previously only available on separate, dedicated, stand-alone units. These multi-function displays allow you to select and view radar, GPS, an electronic chart plotter, depth sounder and other onboard electronics on a single display unit. Usually these displays use a wide, split screen.

Multi-function/networked systems

Although seldom used except aboard the largest of sailboats, networking allows more than one multi-functional display in different locations, such as at the helm, in the cabin at the nav station, or on the fly-bridge of a fishing boat. At each location the display unit can access and control any of the functions available in the system. Most marine electronic manufacturers have their own proprietary networking systems and equipment that allows for future expandability.

Radar overlay

One of the biggest recent advances in today's radars is the chart/radar overlay, in which the radar display is overlaid on a GPS-controlled electronic chart, eliminating many of the problems associated with trying to monitor and interpret separate displays.

Misinterpretation

With any radar, it is of vital importance to spend time using your radar on days with good visibility, to learn the controls, display options, and to compare the appearance of various types of targets on the screen with those seen visually. It cannot be stressed too highly that if you wait for a foggy day to use the radar for the first time, you might be better off not having radar on board at all. Even with trained, professional crews, many ship collisions have resulted from misinterpretation of the radar display—especially in the early days of radar's use at sea. Notably were the collisions of the NECETO DE LORRINAGE with the SITALA, and the CRYSTAL JEWEL with the BRITISH AVIATOR in the English Channel in 1961. The collision of the ANDREA DORIA with the STOCKHOLM in 1956, which sunk the ANDREA DORIA, occurred even though both vessels were monitoring, but misinterpreting, their radar displays.

Chart Plotters

The typical chart plotter consists of a display unit, either black-and-white or color, and a GPS. The plotter displays your boat's position as a symbol superimposed on an electronic chart. This symbol is frequently boat-shaped with a small dot in the center. That dot shows your exact position.

What to look for

Electronic chart plotters come in a wide range of sizes, options and prices and are available as either handheld or fixed-mount. While the sole function of some systems is to provide an electronic chart, the majority are integrated with a GPS receiver. Since there are no universally accepted standards for the chart display, most manufacturers of chart plotters use a proprietary electronic format. Thus, your choice of a manufacturer determines the type of chart, or chart cartridges that can be used, as well as the software, and the display options.

Some of the basic requirements of GPS chart plotters are a fast processor and at least a 12-channel GPS receiver with WAAS to provide a repeatable accuracy of location within about 10 feet. The GPS antenna should be located out in the open, as much as possible, since the short wavelengths and low power of the GPS signals don't pass through metal, fiberglass, or people easily. It is also a good idea to keep the GPS antenna as low as possible, since an antenna mounted high on a mast will go through pitches and rolls that will be interpreted by the chart plotter as changes in velocity and direction.

The LCD raster should be easily viewable in direct sunlight, and the chart display should be capable of being oriented in "north up," "heads up," or "course up." Although units with color displays are considerably more expensive than monochrome, they provide substantially better apparent resolution and, because of the color differences, it is easier to differentiate between land, navigable water, and shoal water.

Most units feature automatic track plotting, so that a track is saved on your outbound and return voyages. At night or during inclement weather, the outbound track can be easily followed for a safe return.

Handheld plotters are often able to save more than 20 routes and 50 waypoints. Fixed units usually can store over 1,000 waypoints. Variable scaling, or the ability to zoom in and out, should also include a scale showing distance in miles, nautical miles, or kilometers. When heading for a waypoint, distance, direction, speed, and estimated time of arrival should be prominently displayed. The ability to measure range and bearing to any point on the chart is also important.

Although nearly all units on the market have a world map imbedded, independent of the local chart chip, these world maps are virtually useless for navigational purposes. Many chart plotters don't use memory cards, but have all the necessary charts programmed into memory.

Formats

There are basically two forms of electronic charts, *raster charts* and *vector charts*. Raster charts are scanned images of NOAA government paper charts, and have some limitations in their electronic capabilities. Vector charts start as scanned images of the NOAA charts, but the data is stored in "layers," which gives the user options in eliminating specific data layers that are not of interest.

In the recreational boating electronic industry, three software formats have come to dominate the chart-plotter market, Garmin's BlueChart, C-Map, and Navionics.

Garmin BlueChart provides a display that looks very similar to your paper charts, but with a single key stroke, additional information on marinas, tides, and hazards is available. In addition, the operator can overlay and store waypoints into the chart display. The BlueChart charts are also available on a CD, from which they can be downloaded into a fixed or handheld plotter from a laptop or desktop computer.

C-Map is a vector-based chart system that provides such features as an alarm when the vessel is approaching shoal waters, and a search mode for locating harbors and services.

Navionics chart cartridges cover large areas, and only 17 are required to cover the entire US coastal and Great Lake waters. Also vector-based, these charts cartridges are available in the "Gold" format for various chart-plotter manufacturers, including Furuno, Lawrence, Raymarine, Northstar, Eagle, and Hummingbird.

Dedicated chart plotters feature only the chart and GPS displays. They are high-resolution LCD displays in either black and white or color, with the vessel's position superimposed on the chart.

Combination chart plotters, which are made by several manufacturers, give the chart and GPS fix, but may also offer more than one service on the same screen. These multi-functional displays (MFD) might include a fish finder, depth sounder, and/or radar. Some manufacturers even have the capability of displaying the picture from an external video camera, or even your favorite movie. In some combination chart plotters the display can also be routed to a remote monitor. Many of these combination chart plotters have the ability to include expanded coverage for future accessories.

Laptop or desktop computers on board can use a variety of PC programs to display charts with excellent resolution onto a screen larger than that available with cockpit chart plotters. The disadvantage is that, with a few expensive exceptions, they are not resistant to spray, are not easily mounted in place, and often cannot be comfortably viewed in direct sunlight. Since these units are usually below deck, they can rarely be seen by the helmsman. For the on-board computer, there are software chart packages available in various formats, and several options are available, such as Offshore Navigator's interface that allows your computer to drive your autopilot.

Prices of chart plotters vary between about $600 for a black-and-white low-end unit, to about $18,000 for a top-of-the-line combination display model.

Wireless technology and solar power for navigational instruments are now expanding in the marketplace. By using radio-frequency signals and built-in solar panels, these new instruments can be installed as either primary or remote monitors with no cables whatsoever.

Depth Sounders

Two thousand years ago, during the age of the Roman Empire, weights were molded from lead to replace the stone tied to a string that had been used previously to measure depths off the side of a ship. This lead line was one of the first navigational instruments, and has remained relatively unchanged for two millennia. It was the only method of measuring depth till the 1930s.

In the 1920s, someone got the brilliant idea of measuring depth by using an echo from the sea bottom. The first attempt was by firing a cartridge into the water on one side of the ship and listening for that sound and the return echo on the other side of the ship. But, since sound travels about four times as fast in water as it does in air, the echo, which returned in milliseconds, was too short a time to measure with the relatively crude technology of that decade. At 24 feet, the sound would be returned in about a hundredth of a second.

The electronic depth sounder

It wasn't till a decade later, when electronics was progressing in leaps and bounds, that echo depth sounding became practical, using an electrical phenomenon known as the piezo-electric effect.

The piezo-electric effect was first discovered in 1880 by scientists Pierre and Jacques Curie. They discovered that if you take certain crystalline substances, such as quartz, put a metal plate on each side of it, and apply a voltage to these metal plates, the crystal physically changes shape. Now, if you put this mechanism under water and hit those electric plates with a sudden, short, high voltage, the crystal changes shape so suddenly that it creates an underwater sound. This sound could then be used to replicate the crude method of firing a cartridge into the water that was used in the 1920s experiment.

This same quartz crystal also works similarly in the reverse direction. If you put pressure on this crystal, a voltage is developed between the two plates, and if tension is applied to the crystal, an opposite voltage is developed. Using this reverse technology, the quartz crystal can be used to receive the return sound (a pressure-wave), which strikes it, and creates a voltage. By measuring the time difference between the sound initiated by applying the sudden voltage between the crystal's two plates, and the voltage generated when the return sound strikes the crystal, and knowing how fast sound travels in water, the depth of the water can be determined. A device that can change energy from one system to another—in this case from electrical energy to sound and vice versa—is known as a transducer. Although the same crystal can be used to both generate and receive the sound waves, in some applications two separate crystals are used.

The problem is that this transducer can pick up other sounds, such as the boat's hull striking the waves, or the sound of the engine. To eliminate these unwanted sounds the voltage impressed on the crystal is via short bursts of an ultrasonic frequency. In the reception mode, the receiver is tuned to only receive this same reflected specific frequency, to the exclusion of all other unwanted sounds.

The sound radiated into the water is in the shape of a cone. This shape is determined by the frequency of the pulsed signal and the physical characteristics of the transducer, and the area of the bottom covered by this cone of sound is a function of depth. A reflection occurs whenever the sound strikes a boundary whose propagation characteristics are different from those of the water into which the sound was transmitted.

Although much of the early experimentation was done with quartz crystals, other crystalline substances are now generally used for the transducer.

Accuracy

So now we have a system for measuring depth that is just as accurate as the lead line—or do we? Sound travels faster as the transmission medium becomes denser. Thus, sound travels about four times faster in water than in air, about 4,800 feet per second. But there are varying densities of water. If you measure a depth using an echo sounder in the Great Lakes, and then measure that same depth off the New England coast, you'll get two different readings. Since the salt water of the Atlantic is denser than the fresh water of the Great Lakes, the sound will travel faster, the return time will be shorter, and the depth finder will indicate a shallower depth. Similarly, if you measure that same depth in the Gulf of Mexico, there will be yet a third reading, since the Gulf of Mexico has lower salinity than the waters off New England. There is always some difference between the actual depth and the depth indicated. Although these differences are relatively minor, often bathymetric depth measurements are still being done by the most accurate method—the 2,000-year-old lead line.

Other factors can also affect the accuracy of the echo depth sounder, such as seaweed or grass, a soft mud bottom, a school of fish or plankton, or a thermocline (a horizontal interface between cold and warm water). Also, since the sound pulses are propagated down in the shape of a cone, the first reflected sound will be interpreted as the depth beneath the boat, when these reflections may actually be coming from objects at the edge of the cone. Another source of error is the heel of a sailboat or rolling of the boat, which causes the transmission cone to become canted. Compensation must also be made for how deep the transducer is below the surface of the water.

The modern depth sounder is much more user-friendly than the old lead line, and is now the instrument of choice on modern sailboats.

Solar Panels

On a bright, sunny day, when directly overhead, the sun supplies about 1,000 watts of energy per square meter. If all the energy across the sun's electromagnetic spectrum could be collected, it wouldn't take a very large solar array to supply all our needs both on shore and on the water.

To convert a portion of this potential energy into electricity, photovoltaic cells (*photo*, meaning light, and *voltaic*, pertaining to electricity) are used. But these systems are usually less than 15% efficient, at the most. In the wide range of wavelengths that reach us from the sun, only a very limited range can be converted into electricity by these cells. In addition, the necessary grid on top of a photovoltaic cell can block some of the incoming light, and the solar panels are made from silicon-based semi-conductors, and silicon is highly reflective.

The cells used in a solar panel are generally constructed of one of several types of impure silicon, and each of these individual cells has a maximum output of about 0.5 volt.

When light, in the form of photons, strikes a cell it knocks electrons loose. These electrons are directed so they create a current flow between the metal contacts at the top and the bottom of the cell and, combined with the cell's electric field, create a voltage from which the cell can produce power.

Types of solar panels

There are three basic types of solar panels available:

> **Monocrystalline** panels are recognizable by their black, round or semi-circular cells, connected by silver wires. Their use has dwindled in recent years.

76

Polycrystalline cells use a different type of manufacturing process. These panels can be recognized by the black, rectangular cells, closely packed together, resembling a tiled wall. Polycrystalline panels can reach about 11% efficiency and are a common product in the solar panel marketplace.

Solar panels of monocrystalline or polycrystalline cells consist of 30-36 individual cells (for a 12-volt system) wired in series.

Amorphous panels are built up as a single unit, with combinations of parallel and series cells and conductors linking them. Amorphous panels, as the name implies, have a monochromatic surface with no apparent individual cell structure. Electrically, they are a combination of series and parallel cells, and typically incorporate numerous by-pass diodes, which give them a distinct advantage where shadows are present. Since amorphous panels only reach 6%-7% efficiency (about half that of monocrystalline and polycrystalline panels), they need to be bigger for a given output.

Amperage available from any solar panel is proportional to the area of each cell. Cost-per-watt of the three panels is about the same, and a rough estimate is that the installation of a solar panel system aboard a boat will run about $6 to $8 per watt, with amorphous panels at the high end of the price range—however the space required is vastly different. For a given power output, the space required for the least efficient amorphous panels is about twice that of the monocrystalline and polycrystalline panels.

All three types of panels, when properly cared for, have a life expectancy of over 20 years. Typically these panels will give about 80% of their rated output when 20 years old.

Panel mounting

Panels should not be in a location where they might be walked on, and they must be firmly attached so that they can't be dislodged by wind or waves.

The performance of a solar panel is highly dependent on the panel's orientation to the sun, the latitude it is operating in, the season of the year, cloud cover, time of day, shadows, and temperature.

Shadows on these panels are a big problem aboard sailboats. With monocrystalline and polycrystalline panels, a cell with a shadow on it not only doesn't contribute power, but it also blocks the power generated by the other cells. The cells in these panels are wired in series, much like a string of Christmas tree bulbs, and when one bulb (or cell) is out, the whole string goes dark.

In mounting solar panels it is best to use framed panels with glass overlays. Particular attention should be given to possible corrosion where the electric wires exit the panels.

Panels facing south, toward the equator (or north, toward the equator in the southern hemisphere) should be tilted at an angle to the horizon equal to their latitude, for best overall results. Modifying this angle, due to the changing declination of the sun throughout the year, is also helpful.

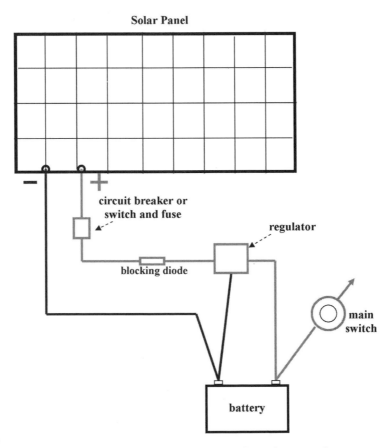

A typical wiring diagram for a single solar panel.
An ammeter can be inserted in the positive line from the
solar panel for monitoring output current

There are solar-panel tracking devices available that perform this function automatically.

Sailboats on a mooring must take into account the direction of the prevailing winds when selecting a panel's orientation.

Electric hookup

The energy from solar panels on boats is stored in batteries. These batteries will last much longer if they aren't overcharged; so a regulator between the solar panels and the battery is necessary. Some panels are described as self-regulating, which is done by decreasing the number of cells in the panel from 36 to 32 or 30. Nevertheless, many batteries have been ruined by this rather crude method of preventing overcharging.

Blocking diodes in the circuit are also necessary to prevent the panel from draining the battery at night or from a boat's alternator feeding into the panel and burning it out. The downside of using blocking diodes is that they reduce the charging voltage to the battery.

A solar panel's output voltage is reduced with a rise in temperature. This is a paradox, since you want the most sunlight possible but, at the same time, the least heat. Thus, solar panels are at their most efficient on cool, sunny days.

Navigation and Boathandling

The Compass

There are many types of compasses that help the mariner determine direction: the electronic flux-gate compass, an electronic magnetic compass; the gyro compass, which is aligned with the earth's axis and shows true north; and the compass displays derived from global positioning satellites. In this discussion, we'll limit ourselves to the non-electronic, magnetic compass—the basic navigational tool that has been in use since before 1100 AD.

Early compasses used a magnetic needle that indicated directions over a fixed card at the bottom of the compass case, but now nearly all boat compasses use a rotating card, with two or more bar magnets fastened beneath the card. In earlier times this card was graduated in 8, 16, or 32 points, but now almost all cards are graduated from 0 to 360 degrees. Some of these cards are inscribed to be viewed from above, and some have edge markings, while other cards combine both displays. The card is balanced on a pivot, frequently jeweled to reduce friction, and the whole assembly is enclosed in a dome filled with liquid to dampen any oscillations of the card due to rough seas (or cannon fire). The greater the diameter of the compass card, the better its stability and visibility.

Variation

Lines of longitude on a chart are always aligned with true north. The direction to the magnetic north varies with location and with time. The difference between magnetic north and true north at any location is termed variation, which is expressed in degrees east or west of true north. But since the magnetic poles are continuously migrating, this variation, for any one position on the face of the Earth, changes year by year. Charts of lines of

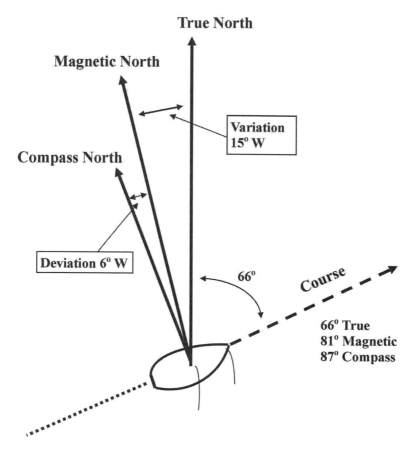

The relationship of deviation and variation to
compass, magnetic, and true headings

equal variation, called isogonic lines, are available for local areas as well as
worldwide.

The nautical chart compass rose

The compass rose on a chart distills all this theoretical information into a
convenient, simple, and usable form. The outer ring of the rose shows bearings to the true north pole—the axis of the Earth, which coincides with the
lines of longitude. The next inner ring of the rose shows magnetic bear-

ings—the true direction to the magnetic north pole. The center ring also shows the variation printed in degrees east or west, along with the date that this change was predicted. This yearly predicted change in variation is only applicable for a few years from the date shown on the chart, since the movement of the magnetic north pole is erratic and unpredictable in the long term, but when using old charts, the yearly change can be extrapolated with reasonable accuracy.

Deviation

Most magnetic compasses aboard boats don't actually point to magnetic north at all, due to other magnetic influences aboard the boat: ferrous

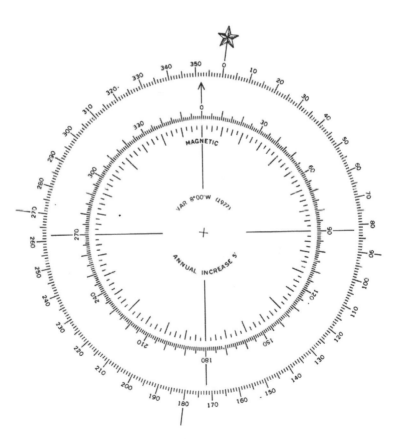

The compass rose

materials, magnets, and electric currents. The difference between the true magnetic heading and the heading that the compass is showing is termed deviation. Because deviation is particular to each boat, this cannot be shown on a chart. To complicate things even more, this deviation changes with the boat's change in direction and its angle of heel.

Thus, the difference between the true heading and the compass reading is the result of both variation and deviation. Since variation is fairly constant at any given location, this can easily be added or subtracted from the compass reading but, for each boat, a deviation table must be created. Creating this table is done by swinging the compass; that is, by turning the boat through 360 degrees and adjusting the small compensating magnets within the compass until the deviation errors are minimized. The resultant, uncorrectable errors are used to create the deviation table. The details of this procedure are usually outlined in the instruction sheet when buying a new compass. They can also be found in such publications as *Chapman Piloting*, but by using GPS instead of the traditional methods, these compensations and adjustments have become a much simpler operation.

With a deviation table for your boat in hand, then the algebraic sum of variation and deviation, applied to the compass reading, will result in the true heading.

Compass styles

The primary mounting styles for boat compasses are binnacle mount; bulkhead mount; flush mount; surface mount; and bracket mount. The type of mount is usually determined by the physical layout of the sailboat's cockpit, as well as the skipper's preference. In addition, there are three basic card types available. For the direct-reading card, the heading is read from the edge of the card. Flat cards are read by looking down inside the compass bowl at the forward edge of the card, and these displays usually also include lubber lines, at 45 and 90 degrees. Dual-reading cards are a combination of direct reading and flat cards, and show the heading either by looking down inside the bowl or by looking at the edge of the card.

Hand bearing

A hand bearing compass is used to measure the direction of a sighted object, relative to the user. These compasses are available either as the "hockey-puck" variety, held close to the eye, or the pistol-grip type, held at arm's length. Both types have a means of sighting that shows the bearing of the target in degrees. The hand bearing compass is not only handy for determining your location, by intersecting lines of position, but is also useful for determining whether you are dragging at anchor, by keeping track of the bearings of features on land that are abeam. It is also good to have as a backup compass for use in the ship's dinghy.

Anchoring

Everyone who owns a boat will have occasion to anchor at one time or another, perhaps when cruising, clamming, fishing, swimming, when visiting friends by water; or during a water-borne vacation. There are many variables when anchoring: the type of anchor; the ground tackle; the composition of the bottom; the type, size, and windage of the boat; the tidal flow, its speed and direction; and the wind speed and direction.

The wind

This last factor, wind speed and direction, makes anchoring a challenge along our coastal waters. On coastal waters the wind usually follows a daily recurring pattern, which is termed diurnal. This daily pattern ordinarily consists of winds being very gentle in the morning then, around 11 am, little cat's paws wrinkle the surface as the sea breeze picks up. Wind speeds from this sea breeze increase till about four in the afternoon, and then begin to die down toward sunset. As any boater knows, these afternoon winds can sometimes become daunting, and much greater than those that were forecast.

This sea breeze along the coast is a very local effect, measured in miles or tens of miles. It is created when the air over the mainland is heated by the sun and rises; then cooler air from over the water blows toward the land to fill in the gap left by that rising air mass, creating the sea breeze. This sea breeze is also modified by the prevailing winds. It will change direction as the day progresses. In the northern hemisphere the Earth's rotation causes this wind to shift clockwise during the day, as it tries to reach what is known as geostrophic equilibrium. (In the southern hemisphere this shift in wind direction is counter-clockwise as the day progresses).

This makes anchoring a challenge. If you've picked a protected anchorage in the late morning or early afternoon, you can be reasonably sure that by late afternoon the sea breeze will have shifted around clockwise, and your anchorage may no longer be protected from wind and waves.

But have you ever wondered, when the wind was trying to blow the paint off your boat, exactly how many pounds of force the wind was exerting on your anchor line?

The American Boat and Yacht Council has developed a handy table with which you can estimate approximately how much holding power in pounds your particular anchor will need in various wind speeds.

Let's say you have a 25-foot boat, and the wind is blowing 30 knots. You will need about 490 lbs. of holding power as a minimum, to keep from dragging the anchor; more, if your boat has more than normal windage.

As the wind speed doubles, the force exerted by the wind on your boat becomes four times greater. For sailboats, or powerboats with a fly-bridge and tuna tower, the wind resistance is dramatically higher because of the larger square-footage exposed to the wind.

The anchor

Boat owners are very defensive when it comes to the type of anchor they use, and they defend their choice of anchor with an almost religious vigor—so I will refrain from entering the fray by not suggesting any specific anchor type. But, generally, manufacturers' ratings for anchors, nylon lines, and chain are dependable. The type of bottom, however, has a profound effect on any anchor's ability to set and hold. Soft mud, for example, can reduce holding ability by as much as 85%. Also be aware that a bargain anchor may not be such a bargain when the wind pipes up.

One of the blessings of modern anchor design is the high holding power compared to anchor weight. This is because, rather than depending upon dead weight, modern anchors are designed to make use of the pull of the boat, together with the forces of wind and wave, to make the anchor bury deeper into the bottom.

The anchor rode

But to do this, we need to let out enough anchor line, termed rode, to allow the anchor to lie nearly flat on the bottom for it to set. Aside from the anchor itself, the angle of pull on the rode is most important.

The length of this rode is expressed as scope. Scope is the ratio between two distances, 1) the length of the anchor rode, and 2) the distance from the sea bed to the deck of the boat at the point of pull. Thus if the distance from the deck of the boat to the sea bed is 10 feet, and we have let out 50 feet of anchor rode, our scope ratio would be 5:1.

Most anchor manufacturers recommend minimum scope ratios between 5:1 and 7:1, but with high winds or a soft bottom, more scope is needed. Below 5:1, the holding power of an anchor falls off very rapidly, so many experts suggest at least a minimum of a 7:1 scope, if you have enough swinging room. Also, in areas of high tides or when storm surges are expected, a respectable scope at low tide can turn into a poor scope when the tide or surge comes in.

Although we have been talking here about anchor line, many boaters insist on using all chain for the anchor rode, since chain has the ultimate chafe-resistance. The reasoning is also that the chain's weight causes a sag, called catenary, and as the boat surges, some of the catenary is taken up, absorbing the shock load.

Research shows that depending entirely on a chain's catenary to absorb shock loads is not recommended. It takes very little energy to make this catenary disappear, leaving the boat at the mercy of what amounts to a solid bar of steel between the anchor and the bow of the boat. And when your bow is connected to the anchor with a solid bar of steel and starts pitching up and down in a chop, something has got to give. This often results in the anchor being yanked out of the bottom. With an all-chain rode, you need a cushioning for those jarring shock loads. A nylon line, with a chain-hook at one end, acting as a snubber, is a simple way to take up these shocks. This snubber line should be of relatively small diameter to provide as much elasticity as possible, since the stretch is inversely proportional to the square of the line's diameter.

An advantage of all chain is that it cannot be cut by sharp rocks or corral, or abraded at the bow chock. In addition, the chain's weight makes the pull on the anchor more horizontal, aiding in the setting process.

Additional factors to consider when using all chain is that it is expensive, has a great propensity for collecting mud, and puts a large weight into the chain locker at the bow of the boat, where it's not wanted. Also, with age, some of the galvanizing will be worn off, and the chain will begin to rust.

Since it's in the heavy blows that we need good shock absorption the most, an anchor rode of 3-strand nylon line provides the best shock absorption, which is derived, not from catenary, but from the line stretching; but an all rope rode will be subject to chafe as it scrapes along the bottom—especially if some of that bottom is rocky. This all nylon rode is also subject to abrasion where it passes through the bow chocks. Nevertheless, nylon has excellent strength and abrasion resistance, and of all the fibers available, nylon has the best shock absorbing ability. At its normal working load of 11% of breaking strength, 3-strand nylon has a 23% elongation rate. At 75% of breaking strength, a 100-foot long section of nylon will become 142 feet long!

Rigger Brion Toss suggests considering Dacron instead of nylon. Although Dacron doesn't have as much of a stretch as nylon, it *does* stretch. Also, nylon loses 10-15% of its strength when wet and becomes less strong than Dacron. Regardless of which material is used, the bow chock it passes through should have the smoothest, largest radius possible, and the line should preferably be protected by chafing gear at this point.

To protect an all-rope rode from bottom abrasion, and to add more weight during the setting process, a section of chain is necessary, and the length of this chain will vary for different regions. For lunch hooks, 6 to 12 feet of chain, as a general rule, is more than enough chain in most anchorages, except where extensive outcroppings of rock or coral may be encountered, but the anchor rode should always include nylon or Dacron line, ideally, as much as possible. For an overnight or storm anchor chain, the length of about half to a full boat length, or an all-chain rode, with an appropriate nylon snubber, is recommended.

When an anchor line is connected to the chain, the chain should be at least ½ the diameter of the nylon line; that is, for a ½" nylon rode, you should use at least ¼" chain. There are several ways of connecting these two components of the anchor rode together. One method is by using an eyesplice and thimble at the end of the nylon rode. A shackle is then used to connect the thimble at the end of the nylon section to the chain. This shackle should be one size larger than the chain. That is, if ¼" chain is being used, use a ⁵⁄₁₆" shackle to attach the nylon line to the chain.

If the anchor hasn't broken loose when this connection reaches the bow chock, you have a problem. So, one trick is to join the rope and chain so that there are no hang-ups as it passes through the bow chock. This can be done using a chain splice, which allows the splice to come through the bow chock so that the chain can be led into the gypsy of the anchor windlass—however this splice can be tricky for the novice.

The anchor sentinel or Kellet

The anchor sentinel has been used by mariners for thousands of years. It is known by many other names throughout the world, the Kellet, Chum, Sent Angel, Rode Rider, or Anchor Weight. Of these various terms, the last one, Anchor Weight, is probably the most descriptive, since this is a weight that is hung from the center, or slightly beyond the center, of the anchor rode to increase an anchor's holding power. Anchor sentinel and Kellet are the two most commonly used names.

This concept for increasing an anchor's holding power is not new. Two thousand years ago those master sailors, the Phoenicians, used this method to improve the ability of their primitive anchors to hold more securely, and the same system is still being used today by knowledgeable sailors. The Phoenicians' catenary stone was the genesis of today's modern anchor sentinel.

An anchor's holding power is greatest when the pull on the anchor rode is horizontal, and as this angle increases from the horizontal, the holding power of the anchor reduces by a surprising and alarming percentage. Royal Navy tests in Britain showed that when the anchor rode is only at the small angle of 10 degrees, the anchor's holding power is already down to about 60 percent, compared with a horizontal pull. At an angle of only 15 degrees, the holding power is down to 40 percent, as is described in the *Admiralty Manual of Seamanship*.

It is the anchor sentinel's function to reduce this angle. Although nothing can correct for improper anchoring technique, the anchor sentinel's advantages are complementary, resulting in greater holding power and decreased arc of swing once the anchor has been properly set.

In John Rousmaniere's book, *The Annapolis Book of Seamanship*, he recommends the sentinel be in the 20-50 lb. (9-23 kg) range. The recommended weight is not only dependent on the boat size, but also on its windage, as well as the ability of the sailor to deploy it easily. Although a very heavy weight would be the ideal, leaning over the bow to attach it to the anchor line presents a limiting factor, and becomes a compromise between a heavy weight and the sailor's ability to deploy it safely. Regardless of the weight, an anchor sentinel should be able to be engaged and disengaged easily, since often, time is of the essence when hauling anchor.

Once an anchor has been set, and the proper length of rode deployed, the anchor sentinel is sent down the anchor rode to about half way or more between the boat's bow and the anchor. A small-diameter warp, or *buddy*

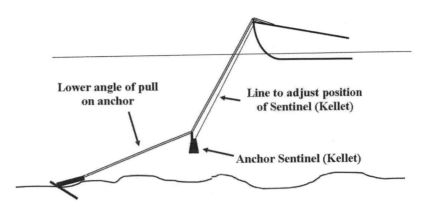

Lower angle of pull on anchor

Line to adjust position of Sentinel (Kellet)

Anchor Sentinel (Kellet)

The deployment of an anchor sentinel

rope, usually a ¼-inch (8 mm) line, is attached to the anchor sentinel to control this distance. When leaving an anchorage the anchor sentinel is brought back on board again, using this warp, before the anchor is weighed.

Anchor sentinels can be used on anchor rodes that are all-chain, rodes that use a short length of chain at the anchor end, or rodes with a rope-to-chain splice. However it's difficult, or sometimes impossible, to use an anchor sentinel where part-way down the anchor rode there is a line-to-chain connection if this connection includes a shackle.

The anchor sentinel itself can take many forms. Some weights are hung from a rode rider (usually bronze) that rides down the anchor rode, while other weights, such as New Zealand's Anchor Buddy have corkscrew slots molded into them enabling them to be twisted on or off the rode. The Anchor Buddy is manufactured for either a rope rode or chain rode.

An anchor sentinel can be a complicated, patented design, or something as simple as a bucket of chain. But whichever type of weight is used, it must ride on the anchor rode without abrading the nylon or rubbing the galvanizing off the chain. Some commercial models have nylon rollers to eliminate chafe and make deployment and retrieving easier.

The anchor sentinel's weight on the rode provides several functions. The sentinel increases the catenary of the anchor rode and keeps the angle of pull on the anchor lower, and in many cases can nearly double the anchor's holding power, since as the angle of pull on the anchor decreases, the holding power increases tremendously. This weight also decreases the hunting of a boat at anchor, and it also acts as a shock-absorber during sudden gusts or wave action. In these cases the weight is lifted while continuing to maintain a fairly constant pull on the anchor as well as on the boat's cleat or windlass.

Chain

There are many options in selecting the chain part of your rode.

Proof Coil chain is made of low carbon steel and is not heat-treated. It is usually designated as Grade-30, which describes its strength, and will usually have G3 cast into each link. Its name comes from subjecting the chain to tensile strengths until it breaks. This is its "proof load." The chain's working load rating is usually 50% of the proof load. Although Proof Coil chain has comparable weight and strength to BBB chain, it is the least expensive of the three types, since there are fewer links per foot.

BBB chain (also known as triple-B) is also a Grade-30 low carbon steel that has not been heat-treated. It can be identified by the 3B cast into each link. It has been the chain of choice for boaters for years, since its added weight creates more of a catenary, and its shorter links have less chance to deform.

High Test (HT) chain is made from high carbon steel that has been heat-treated to increase its strength. It is Grade 43 and has a higher strength/weight ratio than either Proof Coil or BBB chain and has G43 or G4 cast into each link. Its higher strength-to-weight ratio means that for a given strength, there will be less weight in the chain locker. Although it has slightly longer links than BBB chain, many windlass manufacturers specify HT chain as the most compatible to their winches.

All of these chains are galvanized by either the electroplating method, or by hot-dipping, which is preferable because of the thicker zinc coating. Short sections of anchor chain can also be purchased with a thin, polymer coating that not only improves the chain's appearance, but provides some deck protection. Vinyl coatings are also used. This makes the overall chain thicker, but adds much more protection. Unfortunately, with these coatings, it's hard to tell what type of chain is being used, and these coatings have a limited life-span.

Stainless steel anchor chain is also available. It is 316 stainless, is bright and shiny, and has excellent corrosion resistance. For any given size of chain, it is stronger than either of the low carbon steel, galvanized counterparts, Proof Coil or BBB, but not as strong as high carbon HT galvanized chain. It is also considerably more expensive than any of the galvanized chains. It does, however, prevent rust stains on the foredeck, and there is no galvanizing to wear off.

Windlasses

Large anchors, firmly imbedded in the bottom, become almost impossible to break loose by hand, especially after a blow. Of course you can usually motor or sail them out, but that can be tricky if you're sailing solo. In addition, if you are anchored in deep water—more than a boat length—do not motor-out the anchor with the engine in the forward position. This could make the boat over-ride the anchor rode which may foul the propeller. The rule of thumb is that when anchored in deep water, all slack in the rode should be taken up and then you can motor it out in reverse. Still, you're usually left with an anchor very heavy with mud. For larger boats, or for boats with older sailors or those with bad backs, an anchor winch, or windlass, either electric, hydraulic, or manual, and vertical or horizontal, is a great asset.

Most anchor windlasses have a drum, or capstan, for hauling up the line portion of the rode, and a chain gypsy to haul up the chain portion. This chain gypsy has cut-outs that must match the links of the chain being used. So it's necessary, when buying either anchor chain, or a new windlass, to make sure the two are compatible.

When anchoring, many boaters use an anchor buoy, which floats above the anchor and allows the anchor to be retrieved vertically, reducing the pull required enormously. However, one of the problems when using an anchor buoy for an overnight anchorage, is that when there is a tide or wind change during the night, the boat can override the buoy's rode and become tangled in the propeller or rudder.

Dragging anchor

In most waters, 180 degree wind shifts are not unexpected and, added to this, along the coasts there are the reversal of tidal currents, so anchoring for an extended period can cause drastic boat swings while at anchor. But wait a minute! Won't that anchor reset itself automatically following a wind or tide shift? Not necessarily. Of course it may, but you're playing Russian roulette to expect that. The only way to increase your odds substantially is to set two anchors. The most effective anchor plan using two anchors is known as Bahamian mooring.

With this system, the anchored boat can swing through 360 degrees, while effecting the direction of pull on either anchor very little.

There's one further consideration to anchoring in coastal waters— grassy bottoms. Although most of us condemn this grass when it fouls the props of our outboards or for its noxious smell when tossed up on the beach or drawn into the head, bottom grass occupies an important place in the ecology of our waters, providing the necessary breeding grounds for essential parts of the food chain.

Since grass requires light to prosper, it will not be found in deeper water, but this deeper water is not usually where boats are anchored. The problem when anchoring in grass is that the anchor may lodge itself firmly into a clump of grass and seemingly be well set—until the wind picks up and the grass clump is pulled out by the roots. Then the anchor, with its flukes firmly embedded in the clump of grass, will go dragging along the bottom and be impossible to reset without being pulled up and disengaged it from its companion. There's no simple solution for this problem other than trying to make a visual inspection of your anchoring area and picking a bare spot with no grass. This not only preserves the grass, but allows for greater holding power.

The Bahamian moor

With two anchors deployed in a Bahamian moor, the risk of changing the direction of pull on the anchor is greatly reduced when there is a tide or wind change, and the boat's swinging circle is also reduced dramatically. One disadvantage of the Bahamian moor is that your swinging circle may not correspond to other boats anchored nearby. It's also possible that one of your anchor rodes can become tangled in your prop or rudder. In addition, the two rodes can become twisted around each other as the boat swings around, which can be a dangerous situation to be in if you have to move and relocate quickly.

Every time you anchor, tide, wind, waves, and bottom conditions are different and challenging. Although anchoring may often seem to be vexing, the challenge of being faced with a problem and solving it based on your skill and experience is part of the enjoyment of boating. As knowledge and confidence in your boating skills increases, the pleasure of being on the water is also heightened. Safe anchoring is one of those skills.

Preparing for the Big Blow

My very first memory, as a small child, was being in a hurricane in the Atlantic Ocean. Our family was returning by ship from a European vacation. One day before arriving in New York we blundered into a hurricane that was moving up the East Coast. Portholes were knocked out of the side of the ship and our deck was awash with about two feet of water, in which our suitcases sloshed about in our cabin. The ship almost didn't make it. At the New York pier we were greeted by dozens of ambulances for the passengers who had broken arms and legs or skull fractures.

Preparation

June of each year marks the official beginning of the hurricane season; however most of the hurricanes that are spawned in the tropics never find their way to our shores. Intellectually we know that violent storms are a very real possibility, but we usually rationalize with: "It won't happen this year, " and we put them in the back of our minds. However the Big Blow is not necessarily a hurricane. The *Perfect Storm*, the Halloween nor'easter of 1991, caught the forecasters by surprise, and devastated homes and boats throughout the northeast. Strong cold fronts and their associated violent thunderstorms can also have devastating winds, frequently of hurricane strength. No matter where you do your boating, storms are a fact of life. But if you heard a radio announcement that a major storm would hit your area within 24 hours, do you have a plan of action for taking care of your boat? The vast majority of boat owners don't. The time to plan for the onslaught is not when you hear that announcement, the time is now. Obviously our property on land is vulnerable to the winds and storm surge, but even more vulnerable is our floating property.

Boat owners are able to go a long way to help protect their boats, and many of these precautions can be taken when the weather is clear and calm. Begin by checking to see if your deck cleats are adequately through-bolted with substantial back-up plates. Are the cleats large enough to take large-diameter storm lines, with more than one line on the same cleat? Will the chocks also handle these storm lines when they are encased in chafing gear? Do you have large size mooring lines made up to the proper length, with eye-splices that will fit your cleats? All these chores take time, and when a storm is approaching, that's one thing that's in short supply.

On all boats, but especially on sailboats, one of the most important things that can be done is to reduce windage by removing all the sails, especially roller-furling headsails. On small sailboats unstepping the mast is a good idea. For all boats, power as well as sail, dodgers and any other canvas on deck, should be removed. Anything on deck that can't be removed should be lashed down firmly. Vulnerable antennas should be taken off and the plastic instrument gauge covers should be secured with duct tape.

If it is at all possible, boats should be removed from the water and stored on land. An MIT study after Hurricane Gloria found that boats stored ashore were far more likely to survive than boats in the water. If a boat is stored on land it should be well above any possible storm surge and not stored in high-rise storage racks, which are vulnerable to high winds.

You have to prepare for more than the wind. In tidal waters, the storm surge—that sudden rise of water level due to the combination of low pressure and onshore winds—is usually responsible for most of the damage. In addition, open boats must take into account the huge rainfall amounts that accompany hurricanes, nor'easters and thunderstorms. Is your open cockpit self-draining, with nothing loose that can clog the drain? On boats without self-draining cockpits, is the battery charged so that the automatic electric bilge pump can handle the job?

Rivers and man-made canals usually provide good hurricane holes if the boat must remain in the water. Boats in these locations usually survive better than boats at a marina, provided that they are tied properly and are protected from pounding canal bulkheads. A boat kept in the middle of a canal has the best chance; however, this requires cooperation from property owners on both sides of the waterway. During Hurricane Andrew, one boat owner tied his 26' powerboat in the center of a canal using eight ¾" lines, creating a spider web, with his boat in the center. The boat survived without a scratch. Boats fastened to the bulkheads of canals didn't fare as well, due to pounding from wind and waves. If you plan to moor your boat in the middle of a canal, remember that this can block access to late-comers, so the final tie-up probably cannot be done till the last minute.

Fenders and fender boards

Boats secured to a canal bulkhead should employ additional fendering. Usually inflatable fenders just don't do the job, since it's impossible to keep them at the right location, and they frequently collapse from pressure or abrasion. It's a better idea to make up fender boards well in advance, so they can be hung on the sides of the boat to help protect it from pounding.

In addition, one or more anchors deployed out into the waterway will help take some of the strain off the fenders.

One of the biggest problems when a boat is kept at a bulkhead or in a marina is the boat's hull rising above short bulkhead pilings due to the unusually high water level during the storm surge, or from the wave action, or both. When this happens, the boat is frequently impaled on the piling.

In marinas, properly-installed floating docks make fendering and mooring easier. Pilings high enough to be well above the rubrail of boats during the height of the storm surge are a necessity. Wide slips, with pilings

The fender boards we use on our schooner
when we expect a big blow

99

at their outer ends, are also a big advantage in securing a boat that must weather the storm in a marina.

In a slip or at a dock, the bow of the boat should face in the most un-protected, or open-water direction, since this offers the least wind and wave resistance and reduces the chance of waves flooding the cockpit. Boats that have bow-eyes to winch them up on a trailer should make use of them as a strong fastening point. Dockline lengths must be long enough to allow the boat to rise to the maximum expected storm surge (or beyond), and to make it possible to run mooring lines to the farthest point possible. Unfor-tunately, these long line lengths usually mean that a boat in a confined slip has a good chance of rubbing the pilings due to line stretch. Again, fender boards are a big help in this situation.

Lines

Large diameter lines should be installed in place of, or in addition to, the normal mooring lines. Nylon mooring lines are the material of choice, since they provide both strength and a shock-absorbing effect to sudden strains. The down-side of this shock-absorbing protection is that these nylon lines s-t-r-e-t-c-h. At a mere 200 pounds of pressure, a ¼" line, twenty feet long, can stretch four feet or more, while under the same pressure, a ½" line of twenty feet will stretch only about one foot. The rule-of-thumb is that a good quality nylon line will stretch 25% of its length at 50% of its breaking strength. This stretch factor must be taken into account when you are setting up storm lines so that the stretch caused by wind and wave pressure won't allow the boat to pound the dock, the pilings, or an adjoining boat. Remem-ber, larger diameter equals less stretch. Double the diameter and you cut the stretch to one-quarter (the stretch is inversely proportional to the square of the diameter). Also, larger diameter lines are less likely to fail from chafing.

An unexpected finding by MIT after Hurricane Gloria showed that many nylon lines, which were angled across a chock, failed internally when the core melted from the friction created by the repeated stretch cycles. Most high-quality nylon lines are treated with a lubricant to reduce this type of failure, but this lubricant dissipates with the aging of the line. An-other little-known quality of nylon line is that when wet it loses about 15% of its strength (which returns when the line has dried out). Since we are most concerned with strength during storm conditions, when the line is wet, this is another item to factor into the equation of storm-line size. It's also important to know that for lines of equal diameter, a braided line has more strength than a 3-ply line, and colored line has just slightly less strength than natural.

For those boats that weather a storm on a mooring, there are special considerations. Most yacht clubs and marinas prescribe the equipment used on a permanent mooring, so the underwater portion of a mooring is usually beyond the control of the boat owner. However the pendant, or pendants (there should be at least two) from mooring to boat should be checked carefully. Since they go through the bow chocks at a sharp angle they are especially subject to stress and abrasion, and extra chaffing protection is necessary.

When Keith and Gloria Lyman had their boat on a mooring in the Hudson River during a nor'easter, it broke away and went on the rocks. "Although the mooring and pendants were in good condition, there were sharp corners on the bow chocks that eventually sawed through the chafing gear and pendants," Keith recalls. As a chafe preventer, neoprene garden hose or heavy canvas is good insurance.

This brings us to the question of nylon line quality. There is a wide range of differences in nylon lines, with the cheaper nylon stretching more and having considerably less abrasion-resistance and internal lubrication—so don't skimp here. It's much cheaper buying high-quality line than buying a new boat. Insurance companies estimate that up to half of the boat damage due to Hurricane Andrew, that hit Florida in August 1992, could have been prevented with adequate dock lines.

Unfortunately no matter how well you protect your own boat, frequently it's the careless boat owner near you whose boat is poorly tied or breaks loose that can be the cause of your damage. When one boat damages another under these circumstances, insurance companies seldom hold each other liable for damage in an Act-of-God catastrophe. The damage to your boat from the negligence of another owner is the same as if it were our own fault. To help prevent the problem of inadequately tied boats, many marinas and yacht clubs specify minimum line diameters for docklines. It's a rule designed to counter stupidity. It wouldn't hurt to encourage this policy in all marinas and yacht clubs, and boat owners should see that it is enforced, for their own protection. A corollary to this rule should be the requirement of larger sized and additional lines when a storm is predicted.

Rolling sailboats

For sailboat owners, there is another consideration. When sailboats are in adjacent slips there is the possibility of their masts and rigging fouling each other as the boats roll "out of sync." These impacts can eventually break the shrouds and drop the mast on deck or on another boat. It would be nice if there were always a powerboat in slips between sailboats to prevent this from happening, but it's not a perfect world.

If there is no time to find a snug harbor and your boat has to weather a storm at anchor, the best anchoring bottoms, in descending order of holding, are sand, clay, hard mud, shells, and soft mud. Needless to say, the larger the anchors and the more anchors deployed, the better. A BoatUS test found that embedment type anchors, those that are screwed into the bottom, are the most likely to hold.

Roller-furling jibs

The worst knockdown we've ever had—a 90-degree one—occurred several decades ago in the relatively benign waters of the Intracoastal Waterway. With a thunderstorm approaching, we anchored our sloop off-channel and battened down the hatches. I took special care to furl our roller-furling genoa-jib as tightly as possible—so tight, in fact, that there were not enough turns on the furling drum to roll it up completely. This left a handkerchief-sized section of jib out. When the squall line of the thunderstorm hit, the winds, as measured on shore, clocked over 75 mph—hurricane force. We were safely inside the cabin when suddenly we heard a loud snap, and our world turned sideways. The wind had grabbed the small section of jib, and the plastic clam-cleat, that held the furling line, was unable to hold. The furling line ran through the cleat, melting all the teeth, and the genoa came fully out.

What had we done wrong? First, there should have been enough turns on the furling drum to allow the jib to be tightly and completely furled, with two or three turns of jib sheets to complete the job. Second, although clam cleats are frequently convenient while sailing, they should not be relied on in storm situations.

A few years later we observed the same thing happen to another boat in a marina where we were weathering Hurricane Belle. Although we survived the hurricane with no problems, the boat whose genoa unfurled at the height of the storm sustained severe damage.

It's About Time

The concept of latitude and longitude have been known since the earliest days of sail, but without accurate time pieces longitude readings were practically unobtainable, and the instruments for measuring latitude were very crude, at best. Sailors primarily depended on dead reckoning (or ded reckoning, which is a contraction of deduced reckoning) to determine their position. But even dead reckoning required rudimentary time keeping, since to calculate the distance traveled you had to multiply speed by time ($D = S \times T$).

The pendulum mechanism for clocks wasn't invented till 1657, but this type of clock was unusable on a rolling, pitching vessel. Before that, clocks either used a balance wheel or a foliot. Both of these systems were hard-pressed to maintain an accuracy of an hour a day on land. Forget it at sea. Water clocks and sundials were often much more accurate, but both had serious disadvantages on ships; so the sandglass or hourglass became the timepiece of choice aboard ship.

Time signals

The most commonly used sandglass was the half-hour sandglass (although four-hour sandglasses were sometimes also used) and since sailors stood four-hour watches, the half-hour sandglass determined the length of these watches. The ship's boy, or the seaman at the helm, tended the half-hour sandglass. As soon as the sand ran out he would turn it over and strike the ship's bell, adding one bell every half hour till at the end of the four-hour watch it was eight bells. These bells were grouped together in twos, with each group of two signaling an hour. Thus, at two-and-a-half hours into a watch it would be five bells rung as follows:

♫♪ ♫♪ ♪

At eight bells the four-hour watch was finished, the new watch took over, and the process was repeated.

During the 1700s and 1800s whaling voyages and voyages of discovery could last two years or more. For these voyages several sandglasses were part of the ship's inventory. Not because of breakage, always a possibility, but because a sandglass would wear out. Twenty four hours a day the sand was going through the narrow neck of the sandglass from one chamber to another, and sand is an abrasive. After many months of use the narrow glass opening became larger and soon, instead of a half-hour sandglass, it was a 25-minute sandglass. After months at sea a new glass would be brought out and compared with the old one, and if there was an appreciable difference, the old sandglass would be retired.

The announcement of time aboard ship, the ship's bell, is still often used, but on large ocean liners the bell sound is now generated electronically and broadcast on an intercom. Nevertheless many traditional ship's clocks, sold to nautically-minded customers, still chime the four-hour watch bells for telling time.

The standard watch system aboard ship was first established by the British Navy, which mandated six watches each day of four hours each. These watches started at 12, 4, and 8; so if you heard five bells you would know that was 2:30 a.m., 6:30 a.m, 10:30 a.m, 2:30 p.m., 6:30 p.m. or 10:30 p.m.. But to prevent the sailors from always being on the same watch, and to allow both watches to have supper, the watch between 4 p.m. and 8 p.m. (1800 and 2000) was modified into two two-hour watches. The first of these watches, from 4 p.m. to 6 p.m. was called the first dog watch, and the second two-hour watch was called the last dog watch. Although the term dog watch has been used since the 1700s, naval historians are not sure how that term originated.

Each watch was given a name. The watch starting at 8 p.m. (2000) was called the first watch; the midnight watch was called the middle watch; the 4 a.m. watch was the morning watch; the 8 a.m. watch was the forenoon watch; then came the afternoon watch; first dog watch; and last dog watch. The two watch crews aboard ship were often given the names of the port watch and the starboard watch.

John Harrison's chronometer

In the 1700s the search for a reliable method of measuring longitude intensified. Many scientists, because of the large variations in temperature and humidity, coupled with the ship's wild gyrations, believed that it would never be possible to create a ship's clock accurate enough for this task and opted, instead, on finding an astronomical solution. But finally, in 1764, carpenter John Harrison refined his ship's chronometer to an accuracy that resolved this dilemma. Still, these new clocks were rare and expensive and only found aboard government and naval vessels, and it wasn't till well into the 1800s that the average sea captain or packet company could afford a clock that would make determining longitude possible.

In the mid 1900s quartz clocks and wristwatches, which could be purchased for a few dollars, were able to keep time better than the best mechanical timepieces ever made. These watches made practical use of the piezo-electric effect, which was first discovered in 1880 by scientists Pierre and Jacques Curie.

Now, the time from atomic clocks is available to the sailor from several sources:

GPS—Each GPS satellite contains an atomic clock. This time, which is accurate to a small fraction of a second, can be accessed by selecting "Time" from the GPS receiver's menu.

WWV—WWV are the call-letters of one of the radio time-signal stations operated by the *National Institute of Science and Technology Radio Stations*. It started broadcasting time signals in 1923, and its current time signals are based on atomic clock technology with an accuracy of 1 part in 100 billion. The time signals are broadcast from Fort Collins, Colorado on frequencies of 2.5 MHz, 5.0 MHz, 10.0 MHz, 15.0 MHz, and 20.0 MHz.

WWVB—WWVB are the call letters of the radio station in Fort Collins, Colorado that broadcasts atomic-clock time signals on a frequency of 60 kHz.

WWVH—WWVH are the call letters of the radio station in Kauai, Hawaii that broadcasts atomic clock time signals on 2.5 MHz, 5.0 MHz, 10.0 MHz, and 15.0 MHz.

Although the sandglass has long ago been relegated to the mantelpiece, it's still a nostalgic reminder of our nautical past.

Sound-Off!
The Importance of
Fog Signals

Operating your boat in a dense fog can be an anxiety-filled experience. You need to maintain a safe course, check your compass, radar, and chart, set up waypoints, listen for other boats, and keep a sharp lookout for anything emerging from the fog. It's not surprising, then, that few recreational boaters, in this situation, remember to sound a foghorn signal every two minutes, even though that is required by law whenever there is restricted visibility.

In 1972 the International Maritime Organization adopted the *Convention on the International Regulations for Prevention of Collision at Sea.* The regulations adopted by this global convention are known as COLREGS, and have been incorporated in the *Rules of the Road* for the United States and many other countries. Part-D, Rule-35 of these rules defines signals that must be used in or near an area of restricted visibility, whether by day or night. Although we usually consider "restricted visibility" to mean fog, the USCG describes this restriction as "any condition in which visibility is restricted by fog, mist, falling snow, heavy rainstorms, sandstorms, smoke, or any other similar causes." (Darkness is not considered a condition of restricted visibility).

Vessels over 12 meters in length (about 39 feet 4½ inches) are required to sound specific signals under these conditions. For vessels under 12 meters in length these same sound signals are recommended but not required—however those smaller vessels must still use "efficient sound signals at intervals of not more than two minutes," a seeming contradiction.

Although most boaters consider their radar the ultimate method of preventing collision when visibility is restricted, every year a surprising number of collisions occur in fog when both boats were using their radars. Few accidents occur, however, when both boats are using the required sound signals.

The collision of the luxury liners ANDREA DORIA and STOCKHOLM, in which both ships were using their radars, is one of the most notable examples. On the evening of July 25, 1956, the ANDREA DORIA, a day away from her destination in New York City, collided with the outbound Swedish ship STOCKHOLM, south of Nantucket Lightship. Within minutes the ANDREA DORIA was listing 20 degrees and water began pouring over the open tops of her watertight bulkheads, condemning her to a fate similar to that of the TITANIC. Ironically, if neither ship had been using and misinterpreting their radars, it's probable that there would not have been a collision.

The U. S. Coast Guard regulations prescribe certain sound signals, depending on the vessel's operating characteristics. There are different types of signals for a power-driven vessel that's underway; a power-driven vessel that has stopped; a vessel under sail, constrained by her draft, restricted in her ability to maneuver, or towing another vessel; a vessel being towed; a vessel at anchor; a vessel aground; or a distress signal. With this multitude of different signals to contend with, many small boat operators just sound none at all. In a fog this increases the tension even more. While you can expect commercial craft to follow the rules, you never know if there is a recreational vessel operating nearby that is keeping silent. This makes it doubly important that you make your own whereabouts known, so that other boats nearby know of your presence.

Electronic hailers, often found on many powerboats, sometimes have internal circuits that will automatically sound a fog signal. These units are seldom seen aboard sailboats. A few years ago I tried to find a module that would do this same thing for my schooner, but was unsuccessful. I then designed and built a small unit for my boat that would sound the foghorn automatically. It was very basic and built from Radio Shack parts—a one-of-a-kind—but it allowed me to sound proper signals while under sail or power without taking me away from the duties of navigation, listening, and watching.

Just recently this electronic safety void was filled by TSX Products Corp., which came on the market with an automatic foghorn module at a very reasonable price. The *FogMate* is a tiny module, about half the size of a pack of cigarettes. It can be connected to any existing electric horn to send the various sound patterns specified by the USCG. Although the Fog-Mate is designed for boats that already have electric horns, it's not too big a project to add an electric horn to any boat. The module is wired into your electrical system and has several installation configurations, depending on your specific requirements. Installation can even be made without adding any other additional switches, or taking up any additional space on your console. In this configuration the unit is powered from your navigation lights (which should be on whenever you are in a restricted visibility situation) and the automatic horn pattern is selected by hitting the horn button a specific number of times to set the mode of operation.

The FogMate is contained in a flame-retardant ABS plastic case, and the electronic circuit is encapsulated in epoxy, making it waterproof. When activated, except for when the horn is blowing, the unit consumes a minuscule $\%_{000}$ of an ampere, however the horn relay in the module can handle a hefty 20 ampere horn current. The unit can also sound an automated distress sound signal, SOS, which will continue while the crew is preparing to abandon ship.

In a fog there's the remote possibility that you may not hear another boat's fog signal if the timing of that signal happens to coincide with yours. To eliminate this small possibility, the FogMate varies its horn timing randomly between 100 and 120 seconds.

Other manufacturers have come out with similar products.

No matter which system you use, whether you blow your horn manually every two minutes or whether it's done automatically, proper sound signals in restricted visibility situations can be one of the most effective and inexpensive precautions you can take to ensure the safety of you, your crew, and your boat.

The Dinghy

The ideal dinghy doesn't exist. Cruising sailors are looking for a yacht tender that can be easily rowed or sailed (a true displacement hull), and can also be towed behind the mother craft with little pull on the painter (a planning hull). The dinghy must be small and light enough to be easily hoisted and stowed on deck during offshore passages, but large enough to carry the crew and provisions through a nasty chop. It should be beamy enough to make it stable when boarding or unboarding, yet narrow enough to make it easy to row.

The options

Nearly all cruising boats have a dinghy of one type or another. Since about 90% of cruising time is not spent in open water but, rather, in an anchorage or marina, having a practical dinghy that can be easily rowed, motored, or sailed is a great advantage. Many sailors opt for an inflatable dinghy. In fact for many smaller boats, it is the only practical option. Live-aboards and inveterate cruisers who use their dinghies on a day-to-day basis find that their inflatables have a useful life of about three or four years. For the weekend sailor, a good inflatable's life span is much longer, up to ten or fifteen years, if it is well taken care of. Although having an inflatable makes the stowage problem much simpler, inflatables are very hard to row, especially into a wind and chop, and can't be sailed efficiently. One big advantage of the inflatable is that it can be easily towed in open water with its bow fastened up near deck level and only its transom in the water.

A hard dinghy would be ideal, but there must be some provision for carrying a hard dinghy on deck, amidships, or perhaps, on stern davits (not the ideal situation, unless you have a very large boat). This can be a problem on small boats. If a hard dinghy is carried right-side-up on deck, it is much easier to launch and retrieve. It also becomes a good place to stow a boarding ladder, a sailing rig, and oars. Naturally, the drain plug should be removed to drain rain or spray. When a dinghy is stored right-side-up there's always the possibility of heavy seas filling the dinghy, which then can easily weigh a half ton, severely straining its lashings and possibly becoming a lethal weapon, so most cruisers stow their hard dinghy upside-down on deck. Although this is the safer arrangement, it makes launching and retrieving much more difficult. Even if a convenient spot is found on deck for a hard dinghy, visibility is bound to be compromised.

In recent years many hard dinghies have appeared on the market that are made in one-piece from plastic. These dinghies are slightly lighter than their wood or fiberglass counterparts, and have less of a tendency to scuff your topsides.

Many years ago we learned the hard way that a dinghy should never be towed when sailing in open water, especially when the possibility of a storm exists. We were returning from a cruise to Block Island when a nor'easter overtook us, with winds directly astern. Our hard dinghy began surfing down the breaking waves, passing us first on one side, then the other, and occasionally hitting our transom. Soon, however, the breaking waves filled it with water, and it became a very effective sea-anchor. Things were getting so bad that we considered cutting it loose, but we were finally able to limp into the harbor at Port Jefferson, Long Island, at less than one knot. Then and there, we vowed never to tow a dinghy at sea again—even if the weather at the start of the day seemed perfect.

It should be noted that the tendency of a dinghy to surf down a wave can be mitigated somewhat by towing a warp from the stern of the dinghy. Of course this increases drag and the warp is nearly impossible to rig once sea conditions have become rough; and this doesn't eliminate the possibility of the dinghy filling with water. Also, if you rationalize that you'll tow your tender and bring it aboard when sea conditions start to build, it's a scenario that just won't work when the weather begins to turn nasty.

A compromise to the stowing problems of a hard dinghy is having a folding hard dinghy, or a sectional, nesting, hard dinghy. When we're on an offshore cruise, we take an eight-foot folding hard dinghy along on deck. Our folding dinghy is made from mahogany plywood and folds down to four inches thick. We stow the folded dinghy lengthwise on the port side of the cabin top, which doesn't interfere with our visibility from the cockpit.

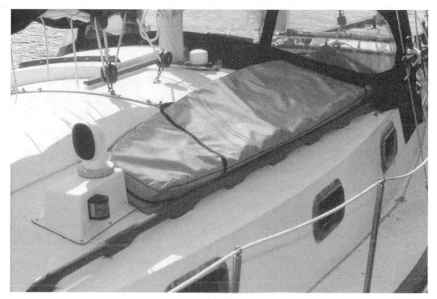

Our folding dinghy is unobtrusive on deck

Assembling our folding mahogany dinghy
on deck and launching it single handed

Our folding dinghy is the *Seahopper*, manufactured in the U.K. and sold by Stowaway Boats (http//www.seahopper.co.uk/index.htm or enquiries@stowawayboats.com). It can be rowed or motored, and also has a sailing rig.

Although we use our folding dinghy when taking bluewater voyages, when in protected waters such as the Intracoastal Waterway, we use our Bauer-10 fiberglass dinghy, which is the top-of-the-line in dinghies and is a very stable boat. Since it is a true displacement hull, it can be rowed easily or powered by a small outboard and with its optional sailing rig it becomes a wonderful sailer. Its ten-foot length and wide beam makes it handy when we have guests onboard to take to a waterside restaurant or swimming beach, or when hauling groceries from shore.

When a hard dinghy is being towed, it should be from the center of a bridle going from the port to starboard stern cleats on the mother boat. The dinghy's painter, fastened to the center of this bridle, should be polypropylene, since a polypropylene line floats and won't foul the propeller. It's best to make eye-splices in polypropylene line, since knots tend to slip. If you'd rather use a nylon or Dacron painter, floats should be attached along the line to prevent it from sinking. (Small, plastic rope-floats are available from West Marine and other marine-supply stores). When towing the dinghy, drag can be reduced slightly by adjusting the length of the rode so that the dinghy rides on the advancing face of the stern wave. But this is usually impossible on a dinghy with displacement-hull lines, since that dinghy will always be riding on the uphill slope of the wave it has created.

Although some dinghies can handle outboards and some have sailing rigs, all dinghies have a set of oars. The ease and pleasure of rowing a small boat is dependent on its hull design, its oars and oarlocks, and the technique of its skipper. Some tenders, such as inflatables, just aren't designed to row easily, and we'll eliminate them from the following rowing discussion. A few dinghies have true displacement-hull designs that allow them to glide effortlessly through the water, however as displacement hulls they resist getting up on a plane, and tend to squat when towed behind the mother boat. But in every dinghy the types of oars and oarlocks, as well as the rowing technique, are contributing factors to a dinghy's practicality.

Not only is a rowing dinghy great for taking out that storm anchor or bringing ice from the marina, but leisurely rowing through an anchorage allows conversations with other boat owners, a social event that's impractical when using an outboard or sailing rig.

112

Oars and Rowing

The one thing common to all dinghies is that they are often, or exclusively, propelled by oars. Many inflatables carry short, awkward, inefficient, aluminum or plastic oars, but for the hard dinghy, proper oars can make all the difference.

Oars

Oars come is many lengths, shapes, and quality. When you visit your local marine store, the chances are that you'll find a good selection of oars, but how do you pick the best? People have argued for years over which wood was the most perfect. Most oars are made from basswood or spruce. There are about a dozen species of basswood, or linden, which grow in the temperate zone of the northern hemisphere. Basswood is the choice of hobbyists, since its wood is light, soft, and easy to carve. Nonetheless, it is tough and durable, and a reasonably good choice for oars.

Spruce is a wood that doesn't rot easily. Spruce is considered the best oar material for recreational rowing, since it is very light, yet has a good strength-to-weight ratio. Sitka spruce grows in moist sites along the coast of British Columbia and can attain heights of 300 feet. Because of the height of the tree's stem, the wood is usually straight-grained, but has a lower resistance to decay than other spruce varieties. For oars, it is light in weight with moderate strength properties.

Oars made from the ash tree are the heaviest and strongest and are the recommended material for hard usage. Ash oars, however, because of their weight, are not as easily used as oars made from lighter weight woods. Ash is the common name of a large variety of trees found in northern North America and Europe. The trees grow to a height of 100-150 feet. Their wood is fine-grained, tough, and hard, ranking next to oak in strength and durability.

Occasionally you'll find oars made from sassafras, maple, or cherry. Oars and paddles made from these woods are prized by their owners since, when varnished, these woods have the look of a fine piece of furniture. These woods tend to make oars a bit more expensive, but sassafras oars are light, flexible, and darken to a rich walnut color as they age.

If you look closely at most oars, you'll find that their blades are often not solid wood but, rather, three pieces glued together (laminated). Occasionally, you'll see oars that are cut out from a single piece of wood. These are more expensive, and the expense is partially a result of the inherent waste involved. While the shaft of laminated oars can usually be made from a 2" x 2" piece of lumber, one-piece oars are made from 2" x 6" boards—so the wood stock costs nearly three times as much.

Blades on most oars are straight, and come in a large variety of shapes and sizes. In the early part of the last century quality oars came with copper tips at the ends of the blades to protect them from wear. Now, this protection usually is epoxy, or sometimes epoxy and fiberglass. Shaw & Tenny of Orono, Maine, who have been manufacturing oars and paddles since the nineteenth century, can supply oars with inlaid cherry tips, a hardwood that not only resists wear but also creates a contrasting touch of class. Other manufacturers, such as Lahnakoski of Finland, use wood wedges that are mortised into the tip of the oar.

Once you have decided on your oar material and construction, length is the next consideration. A rowing dinghy should have the longest oars possible. The rule of thumb is that the length of an oar should be at least 1.5 x beam. That is, for a 4-foot beam, an oar should be at least 6 feet long. For dinghies with very high freeboards, longer oars are required. Many oar manufacturers use the formula that the oar length should be: Beam x 25/14 (to the nearest 6 inches). This would give an oar-length for a dinghy with a 4-foot beam, of 7.14 feet. The controlling factor here is that the oars should be able to be stowed inside the tender for convenience, and as a result some long oars are made in sections. A few rowers (usually those who have grown up rowing racing sculls) prefer to row with the grips of the oars overlapped. In that case, add 6 inches to the above figures.

Oar-maker Shaw & Tenny uses a slightly different formula to calculate oar length. They suggest the following: measure the beam of your boat in inches between oarlocks holes; divide by 2, then add 2 inches; then divide by 7; then multiply by 25. This gives you the oar length in inches, which will have a leverage ratio of about 7:18.

The diameter of the shaft of an oar is dependent on the oar length. Shafts generally vary from 1¾" for the shorter oars to 2½" for the long ones. Although shafts are usually round-shaped and turned on a lathe, square-shaft oars, popularized by R. D. Culler, are also available. With square-shaft oars you'll have to use the pinned-type oarlocks.

The rate of the rowing stroke is proportional to the oar length, with the longer oar resulting in a slower rate. A rate of about 30 strokes per minute seems to be the most comfortable for recreational rowing.

Oar maintenance

Usually oars are sold already varnished, but many oars are also sold as bare wood. Although varnishing allows you to see the condition of the wood, it's a hard job to keep the oars looking good and requires regular maintenance. Paint is more practical, but can hide faults in the wood. Although varnished oars seem to be the norm, I advocate painting oars—or at least the lower part of the oars—with white, marine-grade paint. If you have ever tried to find a pair of varnished oars in the water at night, you'll understand why. Whether the oars are varnished or painted, it's a good idea to leave the grips bare wood. Varnished or painted grips are just too slippery when wet.

Whenever oars are not being used, keep them out of the sun and weather as much as possible. This is especially true if the oars have glued-together (laminated) blades.

Oar protection

When your dinghy is being towed, it's necessary to make sure your oars are secured to prevent loss. Although the oars can be tied down, a better idea is the oar "yoke," which fastens the oars through the seat of a dinghy. This yoke is usually bronze. In the one-piece version it can be fastened in place from under the seat with a clevis pin. When the dinghy is left at a public dock or on the beach, a padlock can be substituted for the clevis pin, discouraging theft or kids' joy-rides. Edson makes a two-piece bronze yoke, where the clevis pin or padlock is above the yoke.

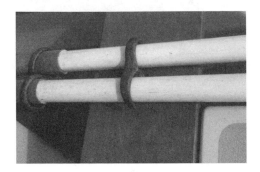

The bronze oar-yoke can
be locked in place to
prevent the dinghy's use

Oarlocks (or rowlocks)

There are many types of oarlocks, or rowlocks, available. For children and rowing novices, the U-shaped, or horn oarlock, with a pin through the oar, sometimes called the North River horn oarlock, is the most common and easy to use. (The term "horn" is usually applied to U-shaped oarlocks, which resemble the horns of a bull). With a pinned oarlock, the pin through the oarlock and oar keeps the oar and oarlock together and the blade vertical. This is not the ideal type for rowing, however, especially when rowing into the wind or chop, when feathering the blade is a great advantage. When I began rowing my own boat, at about five years of age, my father, who had been on the rowing team at Cornell, would not allow pinned oarlocks.

Another type of horn oarlock, extensively used before World War II, was an oarlock where the pin was on the rail and the oarlock horn had a socket in its bottom that fitted over the pin. A variation of the pinned oarlock is the Wynn "Post and Clamp" oarlock, which consists of a metal clamp that bolts around the oar and is attached through a pivot to a post, which fits in the gunwale socket.

U-shaped, unpinned, oarlocks—also a horn-type oarlock—were originally called crutches. These oarlocks are not fastened to the oar, and allow feathering. A big advantage of unpinned oarlocks is that in close quarters, you can pull the oar inboard and still maneuver. Unpinned oarlocks do require practice, however. Unpinned horn oarlocks must be tethered to the boat so that they are not lost overboard, and these oarlocks have holes in their casting for just that purpose. Although a short nylon lanyard will suffice, commercially-available chains with a short bar at the end are also used. Of course this chain and bar cannot be used with top-mounted gunwale sockets. Oarlock materials vary widely: inexpensive "pot" metal, Delrin plastic, galvanized, stainless steel, and bronze.

For the rowing perfectionist, and those with very narrow boats, there are also outrigger oarlock brackets which extend the socket of the oarlock about a foot beyond the side of the dinghy. This type of oarlock, however, is impractical if the rowboat is being used as a tender.

My personal preference is for the round-type oarlock. It becomes part of the oar, and can't be lost overboard. Also, with the round oarlock you can take your hand off the oar without losing it.

As with all unpinned oars, protection for the oar, as well as a "stop," are required. The stop prevents the oar from sliding out into the water if you release your grip, and in round-type oarlocks, it keeps the oarlock connected to the oar. If you are installing round oarlocks on your oars, be sure to slide the oarlocks in place before the "loom" or "stop" is installed. The loom is the raised section on the oar just inside the oarlock. It is often made from leather, wrapped around the oar several times and secured with copper nails. It is this loom that rides against the oarlocks and

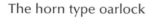
The horn type oarlock

The round oarlock

keeps the oar in place. In place of leather looms, hard-rubber or plastic ones, that can be slipped down over the grip of the oar and pushed down into position, last longer and require less maintenance. The stops should be positioned so that when the oars are held in a horizontal position, the grips of the two oars are almost touching (unless, of course, you like rowing with an overlap grip).

Just outboard of the loom are leather seats, collars, or sleeves, where the oar comes in contact with the oarlock. Leather seats can be installed with contact cement to hold them in place temporarily; then they can be herringbone-stitched or fastened in place with copper nails. Rubber or plastic sleeves are also available. Naturally these sleeves must be installed before the loom or stop. One-piece combination collars and stops are also available in hard rubber or plastic. Since shaft-diameters of oars vary, be sure to check that dimension before ordering rubber or plastic collars and/or stops.

Oarlock sockets, or gunwale sockets, come as top-mount or side-mount and, as with oarlocks, are made in a variety of materials. The Davis oarlock and gunwale socket is a horn oarlock/socket combination where the oarlock can be flipped down out of the way when not in use, but remains attached to the gunwale socket.

Rowing technique

Even though you may have the ideal dinghy and the best of oars and oar-locks, it all comes down to rowing technique. There's not much practice or technique required for oars with pinned oarlocks, but unpinned oars take a little getting used to.

Good rowing technique requires that you use as many muscle groups as possible, not just your arms. With your wrists straight, grasp the oars so that the blades are vertical. Lean well forward with your arms extended in front of you, and put the oar blades in the water with their upper edges just at the surface. Pull on the oars by straightening up your body, keeping your hands level, and using leg power to prevent you from sliding off the seat. Near the end of the stroke, the arms can be flexed for that added measure of blade-distance in the water. During this power stroke the blades should not come out of the water or dip too far below the surface.

When you have completed the power stroke and begin the recovery, feather the oars by rotating your wrists downward so that the blades are al-most parallel to the surface of the water. This feathering reduces wind resistance on the blades, making it easier to row into a strong wind. In a chop it also prevents the oar from hitting the top of a wave. As the oar blades are returned toward the bow of the boat, you should be in the original position, leaning forward with your arms outstretched. Now rotate your wrists upward so that the oars are at 90 degrees to the water, lower the oars into the water and begin your next power stroke.

Keeping on track

To keep on track when rowing, point the dinghy in the direction you want to go, then select some fixed point astern—a point on land, an anchored boat, or a relatively stationary cloud formation, and keep that reference point dead astern. Naturally, you have to look over your shoulder occasionally to make sure there is nothing or no one in your way.

Sculling

There's an alternative to rowing, which is not seen much anymore. It's "sculling," using a single oar astern in replication of a swimming fish. Nearly all dinghies of the nineteenth century and earlier had a notch cut in their transom. The notch was about ¾" wider than the sculling oar. Sculling now is almost a lost art, and few dinghies have a sculling notch in the transom. However, the Pardeys, who have sailed the globe, were able to scull their engineless TALEISIN, of 17,900 pounds-displacement, in and out of harbors and anchorages at about 1½ knots (with no wind), using a sculling oar.

No matter whether hard or soft dinghy, motor, oars, or sail, all cruising sailors agree that a dinghy is a necessary part of the cruising inventory, and rowing easily and efficiently makes using the dinghy a much more pleasant experience.

Logbooks

It wasn't so long ago that aboard sailing ships navigational information was practically non-existent. Cooking was done on stoves fueled with wood, and a good supply of logs, aboard those old sailing ships, was an important part of the provisioning.

In those early days speed through the water and distance traveled were difficult to determine. The most common method of measuring speed, (and consequently distance) was called the Dutchman's Log. The navigator would toss one of the logs that were used for fuel, or a large chip of wood, into the water at the bow of the ship and measure the number of seconds it took for it to reach the stern. Then, knowing the length of the ship, the time-distance formula could be used to calculate the speed ($S = D / T$). The problem was that seconds were difficult to measure—each sailor counted them at a different speed. As a result the Dutchman's Log method was so inaccurate that an experienced seaman might be able to look over the rail at the water going by and estimate speed just about as accurately.

However it was the best technology available, and during that time it became normal practice to record the speed and distance traveled in a journal. Since these speed and distance entries were determined by how fast the log had traveled from bow to stern, the journal became known as the logbook.

From those earliest days of sail logbooks, or deck logs, for recording navigational information, came into regular use, and entries by the officer of the watch were soon required on all commercial, government, and naval vessels. In addition, logbooks were frequently kept by lighthouse keepers, in those long-ago days before automated lighthouses.

Many of the old logbooks that recorded feats that have gone down in history have fortunately survived to this day.

Historical logbooks

In April 1789 the crew of the BOUNTY mutinied and set Captain Bligh and eighteen men adrift in the ship's small open longboat. The logbook of Captain William Bligh's voyage in this small boat across 3618 miles of the Pacific Ocean is, arguably, the most famous logbook in history. It records the amazing voyage in detail, with accurate navigational information and sketches of landfalls. How this log survived the horrendous conditions of that voyage, which lasted nearly two months, with little water damage, is inexplicable.

In another historical logbook, Captain Christopher Jones provides a good explanation of why the MAYFLOWER decided to remain in New England rather than continue the voyage to its destination in Virginia: ". . . we were out of all of our provisions, especially beer."

Logbook entries include such data as weather conditions, currents, courses steered, speed and distance traveled, maintenance carried out, and major events and activities of the ship's personnel, along with any unusual happenings. These logbooks on commercial, government, and naval vessels are considered to be legal documents, when properly executed and signed.

Many recreational craft have also found the practice of keeping a logbook useful and these vessels' logbooks have also often been accepted in court as legal evidence. But, more importantly, these recreational logbooks preserve a diary of past cruises, and record important data and charts that will help when return cruises are made to the same location. Even many very small boats feel that a logbook is a wonderful memoir of their experiences on the water. Arnie and Lexi Janaro kept a logbook for the voyages they took on their 25-foot O'Day sailboat on Long Island Sound, and it's probably no coincidence that Arnie is a Captain William Bligh historian. Their boat's name was BLIGH'S SPIRIT.

Although recreational vessels aren't obliged to keep logbooks, they are a great source of information and pleasure for the boat owner. My own logbooks are a collection of memories that go back half a century. They include sketches of approaches into shoal anchorages, the look and features of distant headlands, some photographs, a record of guests on board, the day's activities, and the all-important weather observations. They are also sprinkled with personal observations and comments—those that wouldn't belong in "real" ships' logs.

For my logbook I stay away from the professional-type with divided columns, each with a specific heading (e.g. position, time, distance traveled, weather and so on). Instead I like a logbook that is more informal and has the look of a journal. I regard my collection of logbooks as part of our family archives, reminding me of past adventures—storms at sea, sunsets at anchor, voyages begun and ended, and those all-important family gatherings and gourmet meals on board.

It is the stuff of memories.

Keeping logbooks on small boats

For small, recreational craft, the journal format is the most practical. The logbook I prefer is from Weems and Plath. It is spiral-bound, with the cover title: "The Ship's Log."

Ink

Since the interior of small boats can occasionally become notoriously wet, use indelible ink.

Storage

Logbooks should be stored in a dry place and, to prevent mildew damage, should be removed from the boat during the lay-up season. I now keep my logbook in a nylon case that contains a hanging file, and folders with titles such as: electronics, electrical diagram, engine routine maintenance, heater, plumbing, stove, etc. This storage case, designed for marine use, also has a compartment for ship's papers and the logbook.

Miscellaneous entries

Most commercial logbooks contain pages in the front for the boat's data: name, horsepower, state license number, home port, owner, hull identification number, and documentation number, as well as other pertinent information on the engine, and propeller specifications. This is a handy, quick reference. Also, there is a section titled Guest Registry for the guests on board.

Speed and Distance Measurements

Today, determining our movement on the face of the earth is as simple as a key stroke on our GPS. We can easily access a read-out of our speed, direction, track, distance to our destination, and estimated time of arrival, as well as a large variety of other navigational information. This explosion of navigational information is only a relatively recent phenomenon.

Measuring speed and distance in the age of sail

In the early days of sail, speed through the water and distance traveled were difficult to determine. The most common method of measuring speed (and consequently distance) was called the Dutchman's Log.

In the late 1500s a better solution for determining speed was developed, the "chip log." The chip log consisted of a half-moon-shaped chip of wood, weighted with lead on the curved side, so that it floated vertically in the water. Attached to this chip was a line with knots tied at intervals that represented one nautical mile per hour for each knot. The chip log was thrown overboard and the line was allowed to run out for, typically, 28 seconds, measured by a sandglass. The line was then hauled back and the seaman would count the number of knots that passed through his hands. If eight knots passed through his hands he would then call out, "eight knots." Well, if you've ever wondered how knots became the term for "nautical miles per hour," there's your answer—they were the actual knots in the string of the chip log.

Another idea for measuring speed was to tow a globe astern. The towline would be attached to a spring-loaded arm which was calibrated in

The chip log provided a reasonably accurate speed measurement.

speed. As the ship's speed increased the pressure on the spring loaded arm pulled it further astern.

In 1730 Henry Pitot came up with the idea of putting an L-shaped glass tube in the water and calibrating it to show how high the water was forced up the tube as speed increased. Although an unpopular idea at the time for use on shipboard, the Pitot tube later became the standard way of measuring air-speed in airplanes worldwide.

By the late 1700s numerous other schemes had been suggested to improve the recording of a ship's speed, but most of these were rejected as impractical.

In 1772 William Foxton patented a log that could measure distance traveled. It consisted of a helical rotor which was towed astern and whose rotating line drove three dials on the stern of the ship which recorded the distance traveled. This, in turn, by measuring elapsed time, could be translated into speed. Since this recording meter was mounted on the stern rail, or taffrail, of the boat, this device was called the taffrail log. Other towed rotors were subsequently developed, but they all suffered the same complaint; the greater the pull there was on the line, the greater was the friction in the dial mechanism on the taffrail and the greater the slip of the rotor.

To eliminate this problem Edward Massey and his nephew Thomas Walker developed a helical log in which the number of rotations were recorded on the log itself. In 1803 Thomas Walker acquired the company, and in 1861 the Walker harpoon log was patented, and used worldwide for the next century. These devices "trolling" behind the ship were the state of the art at the time, even though they were occasionally attacked by pelagic predators.

In the early 1900s speed began being measured with a small paddle wheel that extended below the bottom of the boat. This was a more practical version of the four-foot diameter paddle wheel suggested in 27 B.C. by Roman architect Vitruvius, in which, at each rotation of the paddle wheel's shaft, a pebble would drop into a barrel. Then, by counting the number of pebbles in the barrel and multiplying by the circumference of the paddle wheel, distance could be determined. The awkward invention was never used.

A much smaller, early 1900s, version of the paddle wheel was mounted on a removable transducer that projected through the bottom of the hull. The first models used a mechanical gear to transfer the rotation of the paddle wheel to a recording dial. Later paddle wheels employed small magnets at the tips of the paddles, and as these magnets passed a coil of wire in the hub of the device, they would generate a voltage, which was then transferred to an analog dial that was calibrated for speed. Paddle wheels are still used for measuring speed, but the more modern paddle-wheel logs give a digital readout. These small paddle wheels had a history of picking up seaweed and becoming fouled. This meant that they had to be cleared by diving below the vessel, or through the scary method of pulling the paddle-wheel through-hull transducer out for cleaning, at the risk of flooding the boat.

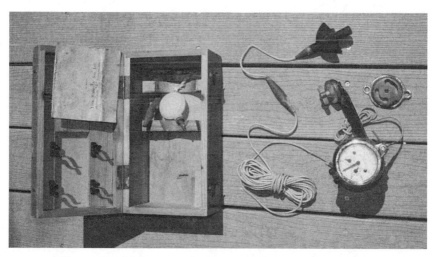

The taffrail log provided the sailor with an accurate measurement of distance traveled through the water

One of the latest developments in determining speed is both non-mechanical and non-fouling. This method uses an electro-magnetic log in which a potential difference is generated in the water due to its movement relative to a magnetic field produced by an electromagnet. The resultant potential difference is sensed by two electrodes mounted in the bottom of the hull; then this voltage is transposed into a digital readout of speed. The advantage of this system is that it is non-fouling, and even the minimal drag of the paddle wheel is eliminated. Still, for those boats that use a separate speed indicator, the paddle-wheel type transducer is the most common speed log on the market today.

But all of these distance and speed indicators measure speed through the water, not across the face of the earth—so the immeasurable effects of ocean currents, such as the Gulf Stream, could cause a large error in calculating the actual speed and distance traveled.

Electronic measurements

When Loran-C became available to the recreational boater, speed across the face of the Earth could finally be measured in real time. This was done by calculating the difference in latitude and longitude traveled over the space of a very short period of time. This could then be translated into speed by the internal computer chip. These calculations became much more accurate with the introduction of the satellite navigation system, GPS. Now GPS with WAAS gives a true reading of speed and distance across the face of the Earth with an accuracy that was undreamed of a half-century ago.

Steering Systems

When it comes to steering a sailboat, even die-hard wheel enthusiasts agree that there is no steering system that is simpler, more affordable, and offers better rudder "feel" than the tiller. Wheel systems, on the other hand, provide power and mechanical-advantage equal to or exceeding that of a tiller, and usually take up less cockpit space. Loads imposed on all steering systems can be extreme, and fittings and fastenings should be commensurate.

Wheels can be mounted on bulkheads, consoles, or pedestals. Pedestals merely contain the sprocket, roller chain, and cables, and lead these cables belowdecks. Pedestals are manufactured from non-magnetic materials such as bronze, aluminum, stainless steel, brass, or fiberglass, and are frequently topped with a binnacle. Engine controls are also often mounted on the pedestal, along with a wheel brake. A brake on any wheel-steering system is important, since it enables the person at the helm to leave for a short time to tend sail. An A-frame pedestal, instead of a vertical steering column, offers benefits in that the steering cables can be led directly down the legs, sometimes eliminating a set of sheaves and their associated friction.

Cable and sheave

There are several basic types of wheel steering systems, the most common being the cable-and-sheave. This system employs a quadrant on the steering shaft that is rotated by 7 x 19 stainless steel cables—type 305 being preferred, because it is non-magnetic. These cables are led from the rudder quadrant through sheaves to the wheel location, where they are fastened to a non-magnetic roller chain that is driven by a sprocket on the wheel shaft.

Radial drive

The radial, or disc drive system, is a modified version of the cable-and-sheave system. The difference is that instead of a quadrant, the rudder-shaft fitting is actually circular, or disk-like. In boats whose configuration allows it, this can often eliminate one pair of sheaves. This, in turn, increases "feel" because of decreased friction.

Mechanical system

The so-called mechanical steering system uses a rod that goes from the base of the steering position to a strut on the steering shaft. This system has excellent feel with precise rudder control and is easily adaptable to accessories such as a second steering station, windvane, or autopilot.

Push-pull steering

Push-pull steering is available in two configurations—double cable or single cable. In the double-cable system two 7x19 cables, contained in a flexible conduit, lead from the steering position to a quadrant on the steering shaft. In this steering system the wheel can be placed nearly anywhere and the cables can be snaked around obstructions between the steering station and the rudder. This makes it particularly practical in center-cockpit boats. The relatively high friction in this system, due to bends in the push-pull cable, limits both feel and response.

The single cable push-pull system is common on powerboats with large outboards as well as some sailboats. With this system a single push-pull cable drives the rudder directly. This system requires a wide transom and is not easily adaptable to double-enders.

Worm gear

Worm gear steering provides little feel and is usually used on long-keel cruising sailboats with heavy rudders, where a large number of turns from stop to stop and feedback from the rudder are not of prime importance. The system is fastened directly to the top of the rudder post. It is extremely reliable, with little to go wrong, and lasts almost forever with just an occasional greasing.

Cable and sheave
steering system.
Courtesy of Ted Tollefson

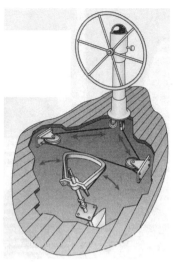

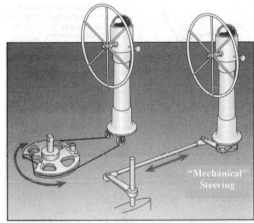

Radial and mechanical
steering systems.
Courtesy of Ted Tollefson

Double-cable and
single-cable
push-pull systems.
Courtesy of Ted Tollefson

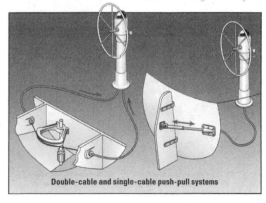

Rack-and-pinion

Rack-and-pinion, the automotive steering system, provides the person at the helm with absolute feel—in fact every wave hitting the rudder will be transmitted to the person steering. This system is also best suited to long-keel cruising sailboats.

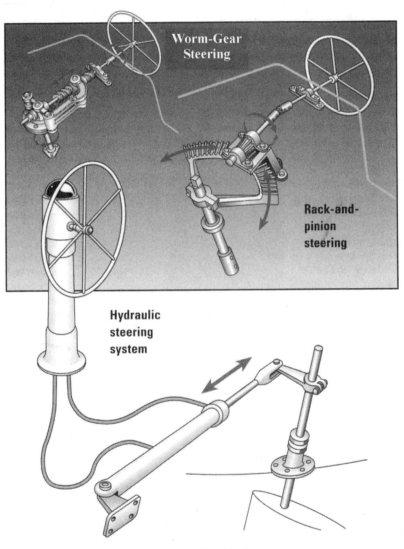

Courtesy of Ted Tollefson

Hydraulic steering

Hydraulic steering systems offer immediate rudder movement without the slack that is inherent in cable systems and, when properly matched to the boat, provide sensitivity and feel. When the wheel is turned a hydraulic pump activates a piston in a hydraulic cylinder; the thrust of this piston is then transferred to the rudder through a short arm on the rudder shaft. With hydraulic systems the wheel can be mounted anywhere and more than one steering position can be used on the same system.

No matter what the steering system, tiller or wheel, provision has to be made for emergency steering if the system becomes disabled. Since backup systems are usually not provided by manufacturers, it's up to the responsible skippers to develop their own practical emergency steering systems, and to try it out before the dreaded day comes when it has to be used.

Engines and Accessory Equipment

The Alternator

Although boats are relatively small and compact, they have the infrastructure of a large city: the waterworks, the sewage disposal plant, and the electrical generating and distribution systems. And just as happens on land, when one of these systems fails, it reminds us how dependent we are on that system's technology.

The loss of dependable electricity aboard your boat can jeopardize your enjoyment as well as your safety. It means the loss of the electric bilge pump, lights (navigational as well as cabin lights), the VHF-FM radio, radar, Loran, and GPS (unless you have handheld ones), and electronic chart systems. Also, and perhaps more importantly, you will probably be unable to start your engine.

Storing electricity

Except for some mega-yachts that have motor generators constantly running, our electrical needs, when away from the dock, are completely supplied from a storage battery, or batteries, which have the capacity to "store" electricity. These batteries, which usually supply about 12 volts of direct current (DC) power, have a finite capacity, and must be kept charged, or supplied, from an outside source.

At a marina, that source can be from a shorepower connection to an onboard battery charger, which converts the shorepower's alternating current, (AC) to the DC required to charge the battery/batteries. On the water, the source of this DC charging power comes from an alternator, which is driven by the engine and rotated by a belt-drive.

An alternator is generically a generator, but not at all the same type of generator that was used in the cars, trucks, planes, and boats of the first half of the 1900s. The majority of the vehicles used for transportation in those days (as well as now) had electrical systems that use DC (direct current). This was dictated by the fact that the heart of the system was a storage battery, which supplied DC for starting, ignition, lights, radio, etc. To keep this battery charged required a DC source, so generators were coupled to the engine to supply this recharging power.

These old-time generators had a rotating armature that supplied the necessary current, which was picked off from that armature with brushes that rubbed against segments of copper to which the wires in the armature were connected. The whole output of the generator went through these vulnerable carbon brushes which, of necessity, had to be quite large. To control the current from these brushes, mechanical, vibrating regulators allowed the battery to be recharged but not overcharged.

The alternator comes of age

But in the 1960s, everything changed. Small, solid-state silicon rectifiers (which only permitted current to flow through them in one direction) allow an entirely different approach to the generation of electricity from an engine, the alternator.

In the early days of the 1960s the alternator was called a "self-rectifying AC generator," which aptly described its function. However it was still a generator, albeit its output was AC (alternating current). The primary difference between the old generators and the new alternators is that in the alternator the current-producing coils are stationary, surrounding the rotating armature, and the mechanical transfer of power through the brushes is eliminated. That's not to say there are no brushes in an alternator, but these brushes are there only to carry the few amperes of field current to the rotating armature, and are not directly in the path of the output. The other major difference is that this new alternator puts out an alternating current rather than the DC of the old generators. Small, powerful, silicon diodes, which are located directly within the housing of the alternator, efficiently and practically convert this AC into the DC necessary for the charging system. Also, the old mechanical regulators, which were prone to failure, were replaced by solid-state ones, which were either incorporated directly into the alternator's housing or as small, separate, outboard units.

We hardly ever think about the alternator on our engines, since it goes about doing its job so well and with few failures. When there is a failure, the alternator is usually easily repaired at a marine-electric shop or a replacement alternator can be purchased and installed with little effort. Although replacement alternators are frequently in stock at marine engine-repair shops, or can be ordered from a distributor, sometimes the name of the alternator changes as it goes from the factory to the distributor—a Motorola alternator may be called a Universal, or Volvo; a Delco alternator may become a Perkins; and a Mitsubishi might go under the name of a Yanmar or Westerbeke.

A boat's battery, then, is like a city's reservoir, and unless that reservoir is periodically supplied with water, it will run dry. The alternator replenishes your boat's electrical reservoir—the battery—and keeps it from running dry.

Ratings

Alternators are rated by how much current (amperage) they can supply. These ratings are for a cool alternator, not one that is operating at a typical temperature of about 200 degrees. The actual maximum alternator output is usually over 25% less than that rating. So, if the alternator on your engine is rated at 40 amps, the reality is that its maximum output is about 25-30 amps. This is important to know, since DC loads on boats are increasing year-by-year as we add additional equipment and accessories to our electrical system.

The output from the alternator is controlled by a regulator, which can either be built into the alternator or be a separate, remote, bulkhead-mounted device. This regulator controls the amount of current that the alternator is supplying to the batteries. Although most regulators are relatively simple, non-adjustable, solid-state devices, for utmost battery-charging efficiency and extended battery life, 3-step regulators are available as replacements or adjuncts to the basic regulators.

Is it working?

The alternator and regulator, then, are the keys to dependable onboard electricity, and that's contingent on being able to run the engine. This, of course, assumes that the alternator and regulator are functioning properly. But how do we know if the alternator and regulator are working? There are many exotic monitoring systems on the market that give complete and complex data on a boat's electrical system, but for many, these are beyond their pocket-book or expertise. For the technically challenged, there is a simple way of checking to see if the alternator is actually supplying the battery with electricity. Using an inexpensive digital voltmeter (analog meters are just not accurate enough), check the voltage of the boat's electrical system when the engine is running.

This check can be made most easily and safely at a cigarette-lighter outlet in the cabin—provided you're not using any lights or appliances at the time. The test is done by placing the voltmeter's probes on the socket's two contacts. For added safety and convenience, or if you're not sure where to check inside the socket, a Radio-Shack cigarette-lighter adapter with test terminals can be used.

This adapter reduces the possibility of accidentally causing a short circuit while testing and, for added safety, it has a built-in, replaceable fuse.

The Radio Shack cigarette-lighter adapter provides easy connections to the boat's 12 volt system

Checking the battery voltage using a cigarette-lighter adapter and an inexpensive digital voltmeter

Simple, shirt-pocket-size digital voltmeters, for this kind of test, can be purchased for less than $20.

If your voltmeter shows a voltage of one or two volts above the battery's normal voltage, you can be reasonably certain that the alternator and regulator are functioning properly and the alternator is supplying electricity which is being stored in the battery. For wet-cell batteries, without the engine running, you will see 12.6 volts for a fully charged battery and 12.2 volts for one that is 50% discharged. For gel-cell batteries, add 0.2 volt to these figures. With the engine running and the battery needing a charge, the voltage should be about 14 volts.

A more professional and accurate check can be made by going directly across the battery terminals, but if you're checking the voltage this way inside the engine compartment, with the engine running, be sure to stay well away from the engine's spinning belts. They can grab you in an instant and be lethal!

For the long-distance cruiser, the ultimate protection from an alternator or regulator failure is having a spare alternator and regulator on board. When on an extended cruise, we keep a spare alternator and regulator on board—and twice in the last 25 years, once from an alternator failure and once from a regulator failure, our onboard spares have allowed us to continue our cruise with only about a half-hour interruption.

Starters

To start either a gasoline or diesel engine, the engine has to be rotated. In a diesel engine this produces the compression that creates the necessary heat for ignition, and allows the injectors to spray fuel into the cylinders. In gasoline engines, this rotation is necessary to draw a gas/air mixture into the cylinders through a carburetor, or actuate the fuel injectors, and also to provide the igniting spark.

A few small engines have hand cranks to accomplish this rotation, but for most of us an electric motor does the job. This electric motor is the starter. This starter motor must be able to couple itself to the engine when required, and then decouple itself automatically. It must also have the power necessary to turn over a large engine and overcome the compression in the cylinders of that engine. This requires huge amounts of current from the battery. Since it's not practical to have an ignition switch that could handle this large current, the ignition switch, instead, energizes a remote relay, normally mounted on or adjacent to the starter. This relay has high-current contacts, and it is actually this relay that supplies power to the starter motor. It is known as the solenoid, and is usually physically mounted on the starter motor. On some starter motors (known as pre-engaging starters) this solenoid has a second important function. When the ignition switch is activated, the solenoid physically engages the gear on the shaft of the starter motor with the gear on the engine's flywheel, as well as providing power to the starter motor.

Other starters (known as inertia starters) use a Bendix-friction clutch to engage the starter with the engine. This Bendix gear operates automatically when the starter motor begins to turn and releases when the engine has started. For this type of starter the solenoid has just the single function of supplying electricity to the starter motor, and the solenoid doesn't necessarily have to be attached to the starter.

The Diesel Engine

Diesel engines are becoming the engines of choice for cruising boats, and with good reason. They have a superior record of reliability, use a safer fuel, produce fewer hazardous exhaust pollutants, have better fuel economy, and are nearly immune to the moisture that plays havoc with the complicated high voltage sparkplug system of their gasoline counterparts.

Even though, in many ways, the operation of a diesel is easier to understand than that of a gasoline engine, many owners tend to look at them as mysterious. But with a basic understanding of its operation, coupled with some tender loving care, a diesel auxiliary engine can provide years, or decades, of trouble-free service.

Rudolf Diesel

When Rudolf Diesel first patented his engine in 1892, it was a revolutionary idea. His engine used the principle of auto-ignition of the fuel. This idea, based on the work of English scientist Robert Boyle (1627-91), was that you could ignite the fuel, not from a spark, but from the heat produced by the compression of the air inside the cylinder. If the compression were great enough, the temperature in the cylinder could be raised enough to ignite the fuel-and-air mixture. In modern diesel engines this compression ratio is between 14:1 to 25:1, which raises the temperature of the air in the cylinder to well above the burning point of the diesel oil that is injected into the cylinder at that critical point, and can reach 1000° F. At that point the diesel fuel is sprayed into the cylinder, though an injector, and since diesel fuel ignites at about 750 degrees F., it will immediately catch fire.

Requirements

Compression, then, is the key to a successfully operating diesel, and to meet the stresses of this compression a diesel engine must be stronger and with closer tolerances than a gasoline engine. This increases the weight and cost of a diesel engine over a gasoline engine of similar horsepower.

Diesel engines have a remarkably long life and reliability, and require very little maintenance. But that minimum maintenance is of utmost importance in sustaining their long, trouble-free life span. A diesel requires clean fuel, clean lubricating oil, and a clean air supply, and any diesel engine owner should be almost fanatical in making sure these cleanliness standards are met. Otherwise the result is shorter trouble-free operating hours and expensive repairs.

The injector on a diesel engine is the most precisely built, expensive, and critical component in the engine. Even microscopic amounts of dirt, water, or bacteria in the fuel supply can ruin the injectors and also score the engine's cylinders and pistons. Clean fuel, treated with a biocide, filtered while filling the tanks, and filtered again by primary and secondary filters, which must be changed regularly, is a requirement that can't be neglected. It has been estimated that 90% of all diesel engine problems are the result of contaminated fuel, so maintaining a clean fuel supply is one of the most important jobs for the diesel owner.

Clean lubricating oil is also essential. Lubricating oils for diesel engines have a prefix C (indicating a compression-ignition engine), while gasoline lubricating oils use the prefix S (for spark ignition). Using the correctly labeled oil in a diesel and changing it frequently are vitally important. Changing the oil often, while the oil is hot, is a job that should be done more often than in a gasoline engine.

And don't neglect the air filter. If dust particles pass through a ruptured air filter, they can score the piston and cylinder walls, accelerating wear and resulting in costly repairs. To prevent a ruptured air filter, these filters should be changed in accordance to the engine manufacturer's schedule.

Diesel engines like to work under a load. Operating a diesel under low loads, such as running the engine for just charging the battery, creates more carbon than normal. This carbon then gums up the piston rings and coats the valves and valve stems. With little load, the engine runs cool and water condenses inside the engine, combining with sulfur in the diesel fuel, and resulting in sulfuric acid, which attacks the engine's internal surfaces. So, low load, low temperature running, should always be avoided.

But even for well-maintained diesels, after years or decades of operation, cylinder walls and piston rings eventually become worn and fouled with deposits and internal parts are attacked by acids, so that they no longer make a good seal. Valves and valve-seats also become pitted and fouled, and don't seal properly. Thus, it becomes much more difficult to get the compression necessary to create the required heat for ignition—especially when the engine block is very cold and rapidly saps away this heat. Injectors also will have become worn and inefficient, compounding the problem. For the owner of an old diesel, difficulty in starting, especially in cold weather, is usually a harbinger of some major repair problems.

Nevertheless, with regular TLC for the fuel supply, lubricating oil, and air intake, your diesel auxiliary will repay you with long years of reliable and trouble-free service.

Repowering

Part 1—The decisions

Chances are your boat is like a member of the family. You could no more dispose of it than sell your only child. But finally the day arrives when you realize that your power plant is on its last legs and there are some important decisions to be made.

Some boat owners don't have a second thought when it comes to replacing their old tried-and-true engine; they go to the boatyard, write a check, and say, "Call me when it's ready." For most of us, however, it's a traumatic moment. After all, repowering an auxiliary is a lot more involved than simply dropping a new outboard onto the transom.

Symptoms of things to come

For diesel engines, the symptoms begin to develop years before things become critical. Whereas your brand new diesel would start within the first turn, now the cranking takes longer—and if the weather is cold—much longer. After a number of years, cylinder walls and piston rings get worn and fouled with deposits so that they no longer make a good seal. Valves and valve-seats have also become pitted and fouled, and don't seal properly. Thus, it becomes much more difficult to get the compression necessary to create the required heat for ignition—especially when the engine block is very cold and rapidly saps away this heat.

New engine versus rebuilding

When the day finally arrives that you realize you have to bite the bullet, there are two options: get the engine rebuilt or buy a new one. If the horsepower of the old engine was perfect, if it pushed you through heavy winds and waves when they were right on the nose and if that engine has always been freshwater-cooled and has not had other serious problems, rebuilding that old engine might be more compelling. Certainly it would be less expensive. But if your present engine is very old and has had raw, saltwater cooling, chances are that having it rebuilt will not be practical. There will be rust, frozen bolts, parts to replace and probably great difficulty in getting those parts. Even though the cost of rebuilding an old engine is typically about half that of a new engine, you may very well be throwing money away on a rebuilding venture. And if you have always felt that you could use just a few more horsepower to get you through those nasty conditions, now is a good time to upgrade.

Costs to consider

Remember that when you decide to go with a new engine there are many more costs involved than just the price of the engine itself. Engines today, which provide the same horsepower as your old engine, are now usually lighter and smaller, and rotate at higher speeds. These smaller dimensions in width, height, and length make it almost a certainty that your engine bed will have to be rebuilt to accommodate the smaller engine, whose mounts will probably be closer together. It's also important to know the type of transmission on your new engine. Basically, there are three different types:

Parallel is a transmission whose propeller-shaft-coupler is in line with, or parallel to the engine's crankshaft.

Angle-Drive is a transmission whose coupler is at a downward angle to the crankshaft.

V-Drive is a version where the transmission is forward of the engine and makes a V-turn to drive a propeller shaft leading aft.

Each of these configurations presents its own problems when rebuilding the engine bed.

The smaller fore-and-aft dimensions will probably also mean that a new and longer prop shaft will have to be installed. Having a new shaft is probably a good idea anyway. After the old engine has been removed and the old shaft has been slid forward, out of its stuffing-box, you'll probably see rings of wear, where the stuffing box (and sediments) have created grooves in the old shaft. In addition, if your old shaft is more than a decade old, you'll probably find that the flange coupling is so frozen onto the shaft with rust, that it is impossible to free it without further ruining the shaft. Also, if you didn't previously have a flexible coupling or Drivesaver, now is a good time to add this item, which will help protect your new transmission in the event of the propeller picking up a piece of wood or a heavy line. If you're already using a flexible coupling between the engine and the shaft, chances are that the bolt holes in this flexible coupling, or Drivesaver, will not match your new engine's coupler, and a new, matching, flexible coupling will have to be purchased.

As for the propeller, there's a 50/50 chance that the new engine may rotate in the opposite direction from the old engine. (If your present engine turns the prop shaft counterclockwise in forward gear, you now have a left-hand prop. If the new engine has a clockwise rotation, you need a new prop.

Even if the direction of rotation of the new and old engines is the same, chances are that engine speed, horsepower, and transmission gear ratio of the new engine will be different from the old. This will probably mean a new propeller of different pitch, diameter, or number of blades—again, making your old prop obsolete.

Most engine installation manuals give charts showing the recommended prop for your particular displacement and hull configuration, and most propeller manufacturers provide a free consultation service to determine the type of new prop you'll need when repowering. Michigan Propellers, for instance, has a Pleasure Boat Prop-it-Right Analysis Form, which will suggest the correct propeller for your new engine.

Occasionally, but not often, on some boats the engine and propeller shaft are deliberately installed at a slight angle off the fore-and-aft centerline of the boat. This is to offset the tendency of a single engine to push the stern to one side or the other—a result of the asymmetric thrust produced by a propeller rotating on an inclined shaft. If your boat has an offset engine, repowering with an engine whose shaft rotates in the same direction as the old engine is much easier than completely gutting and rebuilding the engine bed and installing a new through-hull shaft log.

The smaller engine proportions of a new engine, and the rebuilding of the engine bed will also mean that your present oil-drip pan beneath the engine will no longer fit and a new pan will have to be fabricated and installed.

There is one additional complication of a physically smaller engine that may be overlooked. If you will be using your engine to supply heat to a hot water tank through a heat exchanger, the water connections on the

146

new engine might well be lower than on the previous engine. If the heat-exchanger water lines from the engine to the hot water tank slope upward, an air-lock can develop in the heat-exchanger coil in the hot water tank that will prevent water flow and, consequently, heat exchange. One way to overcome this problem is by installing an expansion tank at the highest point in the water lines at the hot water tank. The pressure cap on this tank should match that of the one on the engine, and filling the water system can be done through the filler cap of the new tank.

Fuel-return line

With diesel engines there's another thing to consider. Some diesels have just one diesel fuel line going from the tank to the engine. Most modern diesels, however, also require a fuel-return line from the engine back to the tank (often called the overflow fuel line). Depending on an engine's particular design, the amount of fuel returned to the tank via this line can vary between an amount that is much more than that which is actually used by the engine, to just a few drops per minute. If you had a single fuel-line engine, the chances are that you don't have a fitting on top of the fuel tank(s) for this new fuel-return (overflow) line. This problem can usually be easily solved by removing the current air-vent fitting at the top of the fuel tank and substituting a T-fitting. One side of this T can then still be used for the air vent while the other side can be used for the fuel-return line. This same problem will be encountered when changing from a gasoline engine to diesel.

It's also likely that with a new engine the water, fuel, and exhaust systems may have to be rebuilt and/or re-sized. Even if this isn't the case, when the old engine is removed, it's a good time to replace those old hoses.

Cost versus value

If you are considering selling your boat within the next few years, it might be tempting to think that the value of the boat will increase enough to offset the money you have put into a new engine and its installation. But, although a boat will be worth more with a new engine, the increase in value will probably not equal your investment when you sell your boat. The same caveat is true if you convert from gas to diesel. But here we are discussing repowering your boat because you want to use it for many more years, not with the idea of selling it.

Professional installation or do-it-yourself

If you have decided to have the job done professionally, there are several preliminary steps to take:

only accept bids from installers that have actually examined your boat,

consider the reputation of the installer and the yard,

ask whether they have installed this type of engine before,

ask for references from owners of boats similar to yours that have had the same job done,

try to make sure that all associated work is specified on the proposal,

make sure that the final installation will conform to the American Boat and Yacht Council (ABYC) standards.

Some boatowners will want to tackle the job themselves. Even if you decide to do the job yourself, it's a good idea to have a professional in your corner, someone who is a dealer for your new engine, has done engine installations, and whom you can trust, can talk to, share ideas with, and order parts from. If you're doing your own work, the closer the yard is to your home the better—again, with the provision that they are ones you trust. And if you don't want to tackle the whole job yourself, you may elect to do just the engine rewiring, the exhaust system, water system, or the fuel system, after the new engine has been installed on its bed and aligned. Whether you have the engine installed by a professional or whether you do it yourself, installation of a new engine requires engineering judgment and highly developed mechanical skills.

We were fortunate that for years there was an engine mechanic near us who would give us excellent and detailed advice whenever we had a do-it-yourself engine job to tackle. Tom Dittamo, owner of Harbor Marine Engines, in Lanoka Harbor, New Jersey, has his business in a marina less than 15 minutes from our home. Tom is also a Yanmar dealer, so we picked that yard, Laurel Harbor Marina, for our haulout and engine replacement. We bought our new engine from Tom six months before beginning our project. He stored it in his shop at the marina during this time, which allowed us to go in for all the necessary measurements whenever we needed to. This enabled us to plan well ahead for our project, and purchase all the ancillary gear necessary. (This early engine purchase, which was suggested by Tom, also saved us 5% on the manufacturer's price increase that went into effect shortly after we bought the engine).

Changing inboard engines is not a simple project. If you are very adept at major projects, if you are a good mechanic, if you have lots of time and patience, and most of all, if you enjoy working on boats and this type of challenge, then you should start doing your homework and putting together a loose-leaf notebook. Begin buying the necessary parts *months* in advance of the expected start-time for the project. I started buying the required conversion gear six months before the start of my project—and that was not too soon. I discovered that the delivery of a new prop would take 6 weeks, and the longer propeller-shaft would take almost as long (it was always, "I'll have it for you next week.").

It's important to learn as much about your new engine as possible before you start the project. There are many engine distributors that have one or two-day seminars specifically targeted for owners of auxiliary engines in general and for your replacement engine in particular. Mack Boring & Parts Company, which sells Yanmar engines and parts, has one and two-day seminars on Yanmar engines that are invaluable. These classes are given at their locations in Union, New Jersey, Wilmington, North Carolina, Middleborough, Massachusetts, and Buffalo Grove, Illinois. The classes cover the theory of operation, explain all the parts of your new engine, cover routine maintenance, and include a hands-on session where you can actually learn how to do routine maintenance and adjust and bleed the engine that you will actually own.

If you do your own installation there are much greater benefits than any money saved. You will end up with an intimate knowledge of your new installation, as well as how all the components come together to provide a reliable propulsion system.

One item that is invaluable in setting up the placement of a new engine on the rebuilt bed, both for the professional as well as the do-it-yourselfer, is an engine jig. This jig, which can usually be rented from engine distributors, consists of a lightweight metal framework that locates the proper position of the engine mounts and shaft alignment. It copies the exact size and angle of the real engine, and can be aligned with the prop-shaft coupling, revealing whether there has to be any change made in the engine bed or mounts long before the engine is swung into position.

The alternate to the engine jig uses another type of alignment method which will be discussed further in Part 2.

Nearly all engine manufacturers have comprehensive installation manuals. For the do-it-yourselfer, this is a must. These manuals, which should be part of your repowering notebook, have step-by-step installation instructions, including alignment procedure, wiring diagrams, engine specifications, dimensions, shaft and prop recommendations, and fuel, water, and exhaust-hose requirements. It's also a good idea to purchase a service manual for your engine. It will be a handy reference for the future, and it gives some installation information that isn't necessarily shown in the installation manual.

The instrument panel

New engines come with their own instrument panels. If you have an instrument panel recess in your cockpit, especially one that is molded into a fiberglass boat, make sure that the new engine's instrument panel will fit into the old recess. If it won't, it might be tempting to try to use the old panel with the new engine, but this usually is asking for a lot of headaches—including replacing the tachometer, oil and temperature gauges and wiring.

Some manufacturers have several panel options of different sizes. Yanmar, in their GM series for auxiliaries, had three different control panels of varying sizes and options available.

Converting from gasoline to diesel

Repowering a boat from a gasoline engine to diesel power includes extra considerations. Diesel engines of the same horsepower are usually physically larger than their gasoline counterparts. After it is determined that a diesel will fit in the engine compartment, engine-bed rebuilding will probably be necessary. Not all gasoline tanks and fuel lines are compatible with diesel fuel and, as mentioned previously, a fuel-return line will also have to be added. The primary water-separator fuel-filter will also need to be replaced. Since the new diesel engine will usually have more torque than the replaced gasoline engine, the prop shaft may have to be increased in size, which, in turn, means a new stuffing-box and prop. Also, as mentioned before, the difference in the rotation speeds between gasoline and diesel engines of the same horsepower will probably require a propeller with different pitch, diameter, or number of blades.

Engine selection

Most of us have a pretty good idea how much power we need, based on the performance of our old engine. The old rule-of-thumb for auxiliaries of 2 hp for every 1,000 lbs. of displacement is usually pretty good. If you really want to get into the calculations, then consult Dave Gerr's *Propeller Handbook* or Skene's *Elements of Yacht Design*. Another source of information is at www.boatdiesel.com on the web. This site, which provides a wealth of information on diesels, requires a $25 membership fee. As a member there are many services available. If you click on Propeller/Power/Shaft Calculations, you can find proper shaft size, power required for a given hull, and recommended propeller specifications.

Be sure to check on the alternator options available for your new engine. If you have high electrical consumption on board, such as refrigeration or a watermaker, be sure that the appropriate alternator output option is specified when ordering the new power plant.

Engines for the auxiliary must, above all else, be reliable. When selecting the manufacturer of your new engine, do your homework. Talk to other sailors who have had an engine replacement recently and get their opinions. Get information from various engine companies and local marine mechanics; check out these engines at boat shows and talk to the manufacturers' reps.

When you're finally back in the water with a new engine, you'll feel much more inclined to take that long cruise you've been delaying for years—safe in the knowledge that you have a new power plant of high reliability for which parts are readily available.

Part 2—Replacing the engine

Although the photographs and text detail the specific procedures on our schooner DELPHINUS, most of the problems we encountered apply generally to all sailboats. In our case we will be replacing a 1980 saltwater-cooled Volvo diesel of 23 hp that had a left-hand prop, with a new 2001 freshwater-cooled Yanmar diesel of 27 hp with a right-hand prop. Although the Yanmar has slightly greater horsepower, it physical dimensions—height, length, and width, as well as weight (200 lbs. less)—are all less than that of the old Volvo. This is common with replacement diesels, due to the improved technology within the last few decades.

Removing the old engine

It would be nice to think that the old engine can be easily removed. In fact, very often when your boat was originally built, the engine in a fiberglass boat was installed before either the deck or the interior mold was in place. The same is also true for wooden boats, where sometimes major destruction is necessary to get the old engine out.

With our boat we discovered that in order to take the old engine out a section of the aft, fiberglass countertop would have to be removed. Even with this cut-out, the old engine had to be canted at a 45-degree angle to get it out of the removable hatch in the cockpit sole. With most sailboats, the engine must be removed by bringing it into the cabin. I had planned to remove the engine's transmission, which would have made removing the old engine much easier, but in trying to do this I discovered one of the four bolts holding the transmission to the engine was frozen in place and nothing I could do would free it.

The preparations

Although our installation was done in the spring, we actually purchased the engine the previous fall. This was done for two reasons: first, we purchased it just before a 5% price increase; second, and more importantly, having the engine on hand for several months before installation was to begin enabled us to check its dimensions, measure the hose sizes, and purchase the hoses well ahead of time, knowing that they would fit.

After all the connections to the old engine are removed (water, fuel, electric, control-cables, and propeller shaft), the screws or bolts holding the engine to the engine bed can be removed and the engine is ready to be hoisted out of the hull. Most marinas have done this many times before and have the equipment and expertise to do the job efficiently. For the die-hard do-it-yourselfer, a hoist will have to be built or, sometimes, the boom can be beefed-up and used.

With the old engine gone, the engine compartment can now be cleaned up and degreased. You might want to consider using Dawn dishwashing soap, which does the job as good or better than anything else. Once the engine compartment has been cleaned up and becomes a more pleasant place to work, the old wiring and plumbing can be removed and reconfigured for the new engine.

When it comes to determining the sizes of fittings on the new engine, you must realize that there are three primary measuring systems in use around the world: 1. metric standards, 2. USA (inch) standards, and 3. British (inch) standards. As the world converts more and more to metric standards, sailboat power plants will increasingly be built to these standards. Fortunately there are many places that can supply metric tools and fittings. But even an engine built to metric standards presents anomalies. Most countries which use metric standards, both in Europe and in Asia, use the British (inch) standard for pipe fittings. I discovered this contradiction when installing my Yanmar engine. Everything on this engine is metric, except for the threads for the water fittings that feed the heat-exchanger for our hot water tank, which are British (inch) standard. Although Yanmar sells the hose adapters that fit these threads, these were not available and on back-order when I started installing my new engine. Luckily, on the Internet I discovered Maryland Metric. They sell a wide range of metric tools and fittings, including British (inch) standard plumbing fittings. They had iron or brass adapter bushings with British (inch) standard tapered ⅜" thread on one end and USA (inch) standard ⅜" pipe-thread on the other. Once these were screwed into the engine block, normal USA fittings could then be used.

Incidentally, Maryland Metric has a wonderful Website describing threads in all three systems. They also have a huge inventory of nuts, bolts, parts, adapters, and metric tools, and couldn't have been nicer and more helpful for my small order of $10 for two adapter bushings.

Another consideration is the direction of prop rotation. Our old Volvo had a left-hand prop, and our new Yanmar had a right-hand rotation, so early on we bought a new right-hand prop (a good thing, since there was a 6-8 week delivery schedule).

We also needed a new and longer prop-shaft due to the shorter length of the Yanmar, as well as a flange-coupling for that shaft. Fortunately, with the old engine out of the way, the old shaft could be removed by sliding it forward, eliminating removing the rudder. Chances are the rubber hose on your shaft log hasn't been replaced in a long time, so now's the time. Better yet, consider buying a dripless shaft log. After removing the old rubber hose and packing gland, I installed a packless shaft seal manufactured by PYI, Inc. This has paid dividends by eliminating the awkward contortions necessary to adjust the nuts on the shaft log. Also, with the engine removed, it was the perfect time to replace our old Raritan water heater, which was then out in the open and easy to remove.

Oil drip pan

In nearly all engine conversions the different size of the engine and the re-built engine beds will probably mean a new oil drip pan beneath the engine will be necessary. I constructed a new one out of fiberglass.

Engine bed

Since the new engine will be physically smaller than the old one, this means that the engine base will have to be rebuilt to match the new engine's dimensions. This may mean that the old engine bed will have to be torn out and a new one installed. This is an important job, and in a fiberglass boat, if you're not well acquainted with fiber glassing, leave it to a professional. We were fortunate that the mounting width of our new Yanmar was ¾" less than the old Volvo, and by installing two heavy-duty ⅜" gauge, 3" x 3" marine-aluminum angle-irons, which were bolted to the old engine bed, we could establish a new and better engine bed of the correct dimensions.

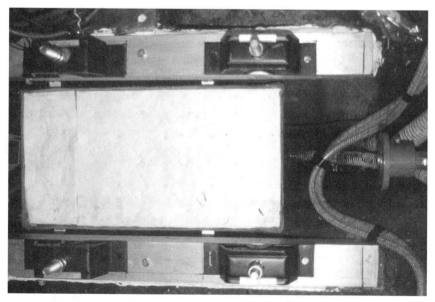

Looking down at the new engine bed. The motor mounts are lag
bolted through the aluminum angle-irons into the oak bed,
and the new drip pan, containing a sheet of Oil-Zorb, is in place

Engine mounts

Most auxiliary engines are installed on mounts that use heavy duty rubber inserts between the top, threaded stud and the base, which is lag bolted to the engine bed. There are usually four mounts, near each corner of the engine, but some engines use a three-mount system, two on either side and one in the front. Both of these systems use nuts and washers on the studs, which can adjust the engine up and down and lock it in place. In addition, the bases of the mounts have slotted holes for the bolts that fasten the mount to the engine bed. These slots allow the engine to be moved sideways so that it lines up perfectly with the propeller-shaft coupling.

When installing the engine mounts, be aware that for many auxiliary engines the engine mounts are different for the front and rear of the engine or for the port and starboard sides, due to the different weight and dynamic loads imposed on them. These shock-absorbing mounts usually have a number molded into their rubber indicating hardness. For engines that require different mounts fore and aft, the installation manual will specify their locations. During the installation, and in the future, keep oil from getting on the rubber sections of the mounts, since it can cause the rubber to deform and swell, resulting in incorrect engine-to-shaft alignment.

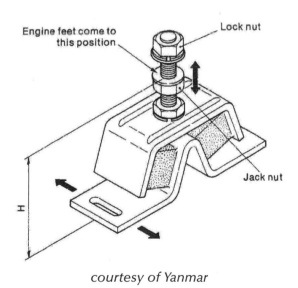

courtesy of Yanmar

Shaft alignment

Shaft alignment is vital for preventing cutless-bearing wear, transmission damage, and vibration. A new engine installation is usually performed on land, and it's important to know that the alignment can change after the boat is back in the water, with the mast stepped and the rigging tensioned. On a new engine this alignment can also change during the first few days or weeks as the rubber in the new engine mounts compresses to its final size.

If you are installing a new engine and retaining your old thru-hull shaft log, the engine coupling flange will have to be lined up perfectly with the flange on the propeller shaft. The engine bed must also have an inclination angle within the allowable limits of the engine mount adjusting screws (jack nuts). Most manufacturers' installation manuals give detailed descriptions of this alignment procedure.

To determine the centerline of the engine, its height, and its inclination, a pointer is bolted to the propeller shaft and a string comes out of the center of the shaft to some point forward. When the propeller shaft is rotated, the location at the end of the string is moved till the pointer circles the string evenly. This string now becomes the centerline extension of the propeller shaft, from which engine-placement measurements can be made.

A similar but simpler way is through the use of an engine-bed alignment jig. Frequently these jigs can be rented from an engine distributor for your particular engine, greatly simplifying the engine-mount placement

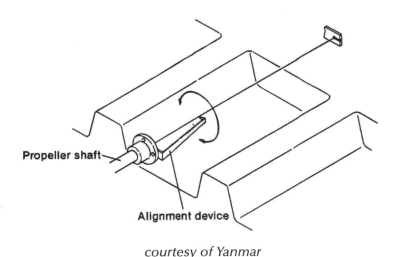

Propeller shaft

Alignment device

courtesy of Yanmar

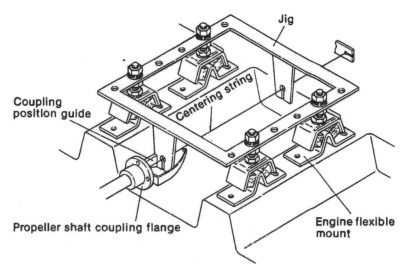

An engine-mounting jig makes engine alignment easier.
Courtesy of Yanmar

measurements. As in the previous step, the string from the center of the propeller shaft passes through alignment holes in the jig, and the engine mounts, which are bolted to the jig, can be located perfectly on the new engine bed, with the assurance that the propeller shaft flange and the engine transmission's flange will match perfectly.

Once the engine mountings have been fixed to the new bed and the engine installed, it's time to check the coupling tolerances between the two flanges. Mismatches between the two surfaces should be able to be compensated for by adjusting the motor mounts. It's not too hard to adjust this alignment so that a feeler gauge run around the periphery between the flanges shows difference of less than $\frac{1}{1000}$ inch. Note that these tolerances should be checked between the flanges themselves and not with a possible intervening flexible-coupler or Drivesaver. Once the flanges match perfectly, the flexible coupling can be added and, with everything lined up, the bolts on the flanges tightened.

Anti-siphon valves

If the raw water output from the engine that goes into the exhaust mixing elbow is below or close to the waterline when the boat is either level or

157

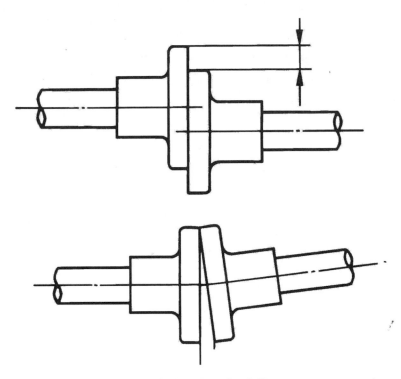

Misalignment may include a height difference, or an angle
difference or, more commonly a combination of both.
Courtesy of Yanmar

heeled, an anti-siphon valve must be added at this point. Without this
valve, after the engine has been shut down, water can continue to siphon
into the exhaust system, eventually backing up into the engine itself and
doing major damage.

Final preparations

When everything has been completed it's time to fill the crankcase and
transmission with the oil specified by the engine manufacturer. Before
doing this, check the levels in the engine and transmission. Many manufacturers ship their engines with oil already added. If the engine uses a heat
exchanger for water cooling this is usually filled with a 50/50 solution of
distilled water and an extended-life antifreeze.

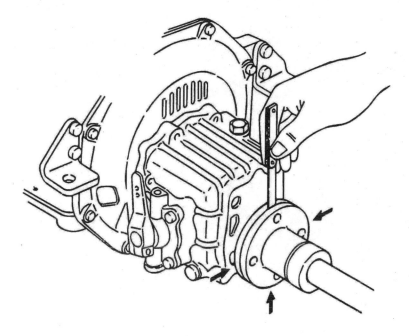

The final adjustments are made with a feeler-gauge.
Courtesy of Yanmar.

For diesel engines it now will be necessary to bleed the fuel system. The engine just won't start otherwise. This bleeding is usually done at two places in the fuel-supply system as well as at the injectors of each cylinder. These locations will vary from manufacturer to manufacturer, and will be described in the owner's manual. Once you have located these points, it's a good idea to paint all of these nuts with white paint. It will make it a lot easier to locate the bleed points when you accidentally run out of fuel and have to do a bleeding job under adverse conditions.

When the engine is run for the first test —no more than a couple of minutes—the levels of oil in the crankcase and transmission, as well as the cooling water level, should be checked, since as these fluids are distributed throughout the engine, levels can drop.

The new engine,
installed and ready to go

Starting and stopping

If your engine hasn't been used for several days, most diesel manufacturers recommend to pre-lubricate it before starting. This is done by pulling out the stop control (on those engines which have a manual control) and turning the engine over with the starter for about 5 seconds. This prevents fuel from entering the engine during the pre-lub process. After the engine has been started it's also a good idea to let the engine run at mid-range for about 5-10 minutes before putting it under load.

Before stopping, let the engine cool down by running it at about 1000 rpm for about 5-10 minutes, then, just before stopping the engine, give it a burst of power to blow out any carbon that may have formed in the cylinders.

The Runaway Plug

Although it happens infrequently, a runaway diesel engine can be scary, destructive, and dangerous. If you overfill the crankcase with oil, have leaky engine seals, have failed turbocharger or supercharger oil seals, motorsail at too much of an angle of heel, have a leaking propane gas cylinder that has not been installed in a properly vented compartment, or have certain mechanical problems, a runaway is a possibility—and when that occurs, the engine speed can easily exceed the engine's maximum red line. Closing the throttle or turning off the fuel supply from the tank will have no effect, since the engine is burning lubricating oil, not diesel fuel. The engine will continue to run out of control, at a very high speed, till it either overheats and seizes, or till it disintegrates.

I've only had a runaway once, about 20 years ago, but that was enough to make me take precautions in case it happens again.

Stopping a runaway

A diesel engine that is running can only be stopped by eliminating the fuel source, the air source, or the compression. The fuel source, such as too much crankcase oil, cannot be easily shut off. If the engine is equipped with compression-release levers, raising these levers will eliminate the compression and stop the engine. Some engine manufacturers, however, warn that lifting the decompression levers when the engine is operating at high speed can cause severe damage. This leaves shutting off the air as the safest alternative (although even using this method, the high suction pressures at the air intake could conceivably cause problems). The suction at the air intake of a runaway engine can be enormous—so don't even *think* about putting your hand over the air intake. A heavy cloth can be shoved into the air intake, or a piece of plywood can cover it, but often, by the time one of these is located, it's too late.

Some Detroit diesels have air flaps that cut off the air, and a few have metal plates that can slide down over the intake, but in the absence of these, another method of cutting off the air supply must be used. A very effective way is to aim a carbon dioxide fire extinguisher into the air inlet, but on many auxiliary engines the air inlet faces aft, making this a difficult feat. You can jam a towel or boat cushion over the air intake, but this can be awkward and take time.

On our schooner, just inside the engine compartment door and within easy reach from inside the cabin, I have a small wooden rack that holds a rubber plug that fits into the engine's air intake. In case of a runaway, it can be rapidly and safely inserted in the air intake, hopefully before any major engine damage can occur.

This rubber plug, which was purchased at a local hardware store, also serves a dual purpose. Most engine manufacturers recommend that rubber plugs be inserted in the engine's air intake and exhaust ports during the winter layup season to prevent condensation from forming inside the engine due to cold, winter air, so my runaway plug also serves that purpose as well.

And just in case I forget to remove the rubber air intake and exhaust plugs during spring commissioning, I have a sign in front of the engine control panel to remind me.

The Emergency Start Button

Many diesel engines have compression-release or decompression levers on top of the engine for each cylinder. As their name implies, these levers hold open the engine valves and prevent normal compression within the cylinders. Although seldom used, they can become very important when you find that your batteries don't have enough juice to turn over the engine for starting.

Compression-release starting

Since diesel engines have very high compression, they require lots of amperage from the battery to turn them over. If the batteries are too low for the job, or if they and the engine are very cold (cold batteries have less cranking capacity and a cold engine is harder to rotate) you're left stranded, unless your engine has decompression levers. By opening these levers, and eliminating engine compression, the engine can usually be turned over by the starter very easily, even when the battery is very low. Then, once the flywheel is rotating at a decent speed, and while still holding in the starter button, a compression-release lever on one of the cylinders can be returned to normal. Usually this cylinder will start the engine running, and the levers on the other cylinder(s) can then be thrown into the compression position.

The trouble is, to do this requires more than one person. One crewmember must be in the cockpit, operating the ignition key or starter button, and another has to be next to the engine to throw the compression-release levers at the proper time.

Solution

Since I frequently singlehand my boat, I have installed an emergency starter button inside the engine compartment next to the engine. This back-up starter button can be operated with one hand while the other hand is on the decompression levers. This push-button type momentary switch is wired across (in parallel with) the engine control panel's starter button (if there is one) or across the starter terminals of the key switch.

Bilge Pumps

There is an enormous variety of bilge pumps on the market. Some are electric, some manual, and some are belt-driven from the engine. Bilge pumps are designed to get rid of the routine water that enters the bilge from a dripping stuffing box, water that comes down into the cabin through keel-stepped masts, or rain or spray that enters the cabin through hatches or ports, but virtually no bilge pump is large enough to keep up with a catastrophic leak caused by hull damage.

Regardless of the type of pump that is used, it won't be able to do its job if the bilge is full of foreign matter such as sawdust, wood shavings, or other debris. A little oil in the bilge can coagulate this foreign material and make things even worse. Although regular cleaning of the bilge is not the most pleasant of jobs, it's a necessity if the bilge pump is to operate properly. Even with relatively clean bilges, a strainer is necessary. This strainer should have the largest area possible, at least twice the suction hose area, but the holes in the strainer should be small.

Nearly all cruising sailboats have an automatic electric bilge pump, and at least one manual pump as a backup. However, for offshore racing sailboats, race requirements usually specify two permanently installed manual pumps, one in the cockpit and one down below.

Considerations

Electric, centrifugal pumps, are low cost, easily installed, and move a good amount of water. The general rule is: use the largest electric pump that is practical. When purchasing an electric bilge pump, some of things to consider are: Is it self-priming? Can it be run dry? Is it submersible? Will it be able to lift the water to the desired height?

Installation usually includes an automatic switch that will actuate the pump when there is water in the bilge. These switches, especially on small pumps, are often integral with, and mounted on, the pump. On larger pumps the switches are separate.

A large variety of automatic switches is available, such as the simple open float switch, which is prone to jam when there is debris in the bilge or the enclosed float switch, that usually eliminate the jamming problem. There are solid-state non-mechanical switches that operate in diverse ways, such as sensing the water level by sonar, or by using differential field sensors. Some of these solid-state switches have an extended running feature, which lets the pump run for several seconds beyond the time of normal shut-off. This is handy for boats with small bilges, where return water from the discharge hose, after the pump turns off, can make the pump cycle again.

All electrical connections to a bilge pump should be with connectors with waterproof heat-shrink sleeves. It's important that electric bilge pumps be on their own electrical circuit, protected by a fuse or circuit breaker with the recommended amperage printed on the pump, and using properly sized wire. When a pump is not fused properly, a jammed float switch can cause it to run continuously, without water. Overheating, in such a scenario, has been the cause of many boat fires.

Boats that are left unattended for long periods often power the automatic bilge pump directly from the battery, bypassing the main electrical panel, which can then be turned off when the boat is left unattended. This practice is acceptable, provided that the pump is protected with a fuse or circuit breaker of proper size.

Checking on the pump's cycling

Unfortunately, automatic bilge pumps have a flaw that can lull the boat owner into a false sense of security. With an automatic pump, every time you check your bilge you see no increase in the water level—even though a cracked hose, severely dripping stuffing box, or leaking seacock may be constantly dumping water into the bilge. To alert you to this problem, a cycle-counter, with reset button, such as those available at many marine-supply stores, will let you know if the bilge pump is cycling on more often than normal. A light and/or buzzer will also do the job for liveaboards.

Needless to say, automatic electric pumps will only operate if the electrical system is functioning, so at least one manual pump should also be available. The most common manual pump is the diaphragm pump, which

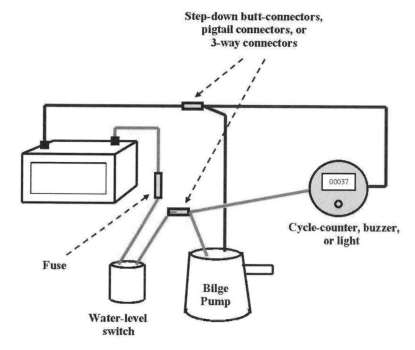

Step-down butt-connectors, pigtail connectors, or 3-way connectors

00037

Cycle-counter, buzzer, or light

Fuse

Bilge Pump

Water-level switch

A basic bilge-pump wiring diagram. There are many variations

is able to move a large amount of water, and can pass small debris without clogging. These may be either permanently mounted or mounted on a board and stowed away for emergencies. A permanently mounted cockpit pump should have the handle within reach of the helmsman.

The discharge hose from any bilge pump should have a smooth interior to reduce friction. Most bilge pumps discharge through the transom or through the side of the hull well above the waterline; but remember, the higher the water has to be lifted, the less efficient the pump. Sometimes bilge pumps discharge into a self-draining cockpit or onto the deck. In these cases, however, any oil in the bilge can create a hazardous walking surface. If there's any possibility of water coming back through the discharge hose when the boat is heeled, a loop can be used, an external neoprene flap, or a one way valve (however, a one-way valve is very prone to clogging).

Finally, a reliance on bilge pumps is not a substitute for checking all your underwater fittings on a regular basis.

Seacocks

The hull of a boat is designed to keep the water out, but most boats also have through-hull fittings and seacocks, which are designed to allow water to enter the boat safely. BoatUS reports, however, that seacocks are responsible for a large percentage of the sinkings that occur every year.

Options

Seacocks are metal or plastic valves that are screwed onto through-hull fittings. They can be opened or closed to allow you to control movement of fluids either way through the hull. There are three basic types of seacocks on the market: the traditional bronze tapered-plug seacock, with a handle that rotates 90 degrees between open and closed;

The traditional tapered plug seacock.
Courtesy of Ted Tollefson

ball-valve seacocks, also with a handle that rotates 90 degrees between open and closed;

and gate valves, which require several rotations of the handle to open or close.

A ball valve seacock.
Courtesy of Ted Tollefson

A gate valve seacock.
Courtesy of Ted Tollefson

The traditional material for seacocks has always been bronze, but there are also non-metallic ones available. Although many sailors are skeptical about these "plastic" seacocks, the best ones, such as those made from reinforced nylon, marketed under the name Marelon, have enormous tensile strengths. For owners of steel or aluminum boats, these non-metallic seacocks eliminate the corrosion problem caused by the galvanic action of dissimilar metals.

If gate valves are used, they should be bronze, not brass, but even the bronze ones usually include parts, such as the stem, of dissimilar metals, inviting trouble. Another problem with gate valves is that they do not have a positive action; that is, you can never be sure if they are completely closed or whether there might be a foreign object lodged inside. Also, they usually don't have large flanges that can be secured directly to the hull, and are thus more subject to being broken off accidentally.

Installing a seacock

All seacocks should be mounted with a backing plate, or hull-reinforcement. Wood backing plates should not be used with synthetic seacocks, since the wood's expansion can strain the plastic. Also, whenever a through-hull is installed on a cored hull, the soft core must be cut away between the fiberglass layers, and the void filled with epoxy and fiberglass, to increase the compression strength of the area where the through-hull will be mounted.

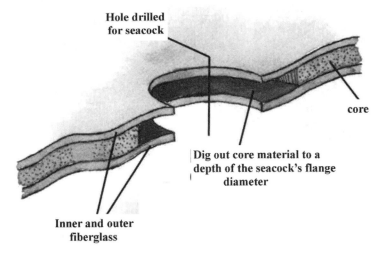

Hole drilled for seacock

core

Dig out core material to a depth of the seacock's flange diameter

Inner and outer fiberglass

Preparing a cored hull for seacock installation.
Courtesy of Ted Tollefson

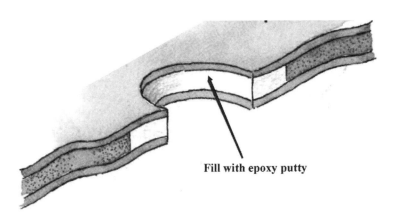

Fill with epoxy putty

The cored hull has been reinforced with epoxy.
Courtesy of Ted Tollefson

The mushroom part of the through-hull, that is, the part that is on the exterior of the hull, screws into the seacock, which is inside the hull. The threads on this mushroom may be either straight, termed NPS for National Pipe Straight (sometimes called parallel threads), or tapered, termed NPT for National Pipe Tapered. When installing a seacock, be sure that the thread type on the outside through-hull fitting matches that of the seacock thread. The same holds true for the threads on the top part of the seacock, which join the seacock to a hose tailpiece or strainer.

Only heavy-duty reinforced hose should be fastened to seacocks and it must be secured with two stainless-steel clamps, since ice inside the hose can exert enormous pressure and easily lift a single-clamped hose off the seacock tailpiece. As for those clamps, be sure you get them at a reputable marine-supply store. Very often those purchased at a hardware

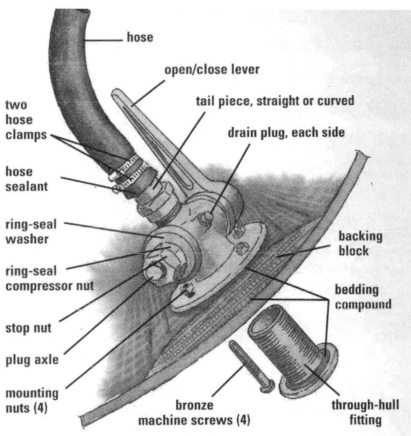

hose

open/close lever

two hose clamps

tail piece, straight or curved

drain plug, each side

hose sealant

ring-seal washer

backing block

ring-seal compressor nut

bedding compound

stop nut

plug axle

mounting nuts (4)

bronze machine screws (4)

through-hull fitting

All seacocks should be through-bolted to the hull,
with a block of wood, or other material, on the inside
of the hull to distribute the load.
Courtesy of Ted Tollefson

store will be labeled "stainless steel," but only the band is stainless and very soon you'll find the screw mechanism rusted, weakened, and unusable. All through-hulls, except for the cockpit drains, should be closed whenever you leave your boat.

The emergency plug

A selection of tapered softwood plugs should be kept on board. These can be used to stop the water flow from a deteriorated hose and inoperable seacock, or they can be pounded into place should there be a catastrophic seacock failure. If such a failure occurs, there's not much time to react. A 1½" hole, 2 feet below the water line, will gush over 70 gallons of water a minute into the hull! For this reason it's a good idea to tether a wood plug of the proper size to each seacock, so they'll be readily available if needed.

Most tapered plug seacocks tend to become hard to rotate if they haven't been used in many months. To prevent this seizing, they should be worked open and shut occasionally. (To make it easier to remember, I make it a point to exercise mine the first week of every month).

Servicing

All seacocks should be serviced annually. Follow the manufacturer's recommendations. For ball-valve seacocks, just a small amount of grease is necessary. For tapered-plug seacocks. disassembly, inspection, cleaning, and regreasing with a waterproof grease should be an annual task. Special seacock grease works better than an automotive grease. Occasionally you'll find that sand or mud may have scored the tapered plug. For light scoring, smooth out the scratches with an emery cloth. For heavy grooves, apply a valve-grinding compound, and rotate the plug inside its housing until it fits snugly; then thoroughly clean both parts and regrease. Since tapered-plug seacocks depend on this grease for their watertightness, they should be greased liberally.

Finally, avoid using a seacock to supply water to both an engine as well as a saltwater galley pump, air conditioner, or watermaker. If this is done, very often the suction of an engine operating at high speed will draw air back through that second device and decrease the engine's cooling capacity. This use of a "manifold" to supply more than one source from a single seacock has been the cause of many perplexing engine-cooling problems.

The Shaft Log

A shaft log guides the propeller shaft through the hull while keeping watertight integrity. It consists of two parts, a watertight seal and a bearing that supports the shaft. When inboard engines were initially installed in early wooden boats, the shaft exited through the stern post, and relied on a reasonably tight fit between the wood and propeller shaft to keep the water out. But since this usually meant regular pumping of the bilge, a better solution, the stuffing box and cutless bearing came into widespread use.

The stuffing box

The stuffing box—sometimes called the packing gland—eliminated most of the leakage around the shaft by compressing stuffing, or grease-impregnated flax packing, tightly around the shaft. Some stuffing boxes have grease fittings, so this grease can be easily replaced. The stuffing, which is a square, plaited material, usually flax, comes in various sizes to match your stuffing box. This flax is now usually impregnated with paraffin or Teflon. To keep the stuffing box cool and lubricated, a small amount of water from outside the hull is allowed passage through this compression seal. This cooling water should consist of about one drop every ten seconds, when the shaft is rotating. Although there is some disagreement as to the drip rate, the rule of thumb is that the stuffing box should feel warm, but never hot, after prolonged use.

Although the stuffing box should not drip water when the shaft is not turning, this, of course, is only an ideal. Few stuffing boxes meet this level of perfection, so when a boat is left for long periods of time, an automatic bilge pump is often necessary. Eventually, the packing in the stuffing box gets worn away and has to be replaced. To do this the old, hardened packing

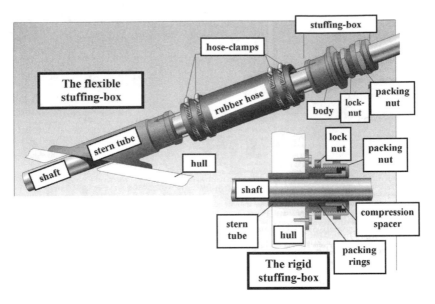

In the expanded view of the flexible stuffing-box (above),
as well as the rigid stuffing-box (right), the cutless bearings
may either be integral in the stern tube or in an external strut.
Courtesy of Ted Tollefson

must be removed. Special tools are available for this purpose. The stuffing box can then be cleaned and new packing installed. When the vessel is back in the water again, the drip rate must be checked, and the compression nut adjusted as necessary. This drip rate should be checked again during the next few times out.

There is also self-lubricating, low-friction packing available. A clay-like compound is inserted in the stuffing box and compressed by rings of conventional packing. Then the packing compression nut can be adjusted so there are no drips. Although more expensive than conventional packing, after the initial adjustment this system rarely needs readjustment.

There are two basic styles of stuffing boxes, rigid and flexible. In the rigid style the stuffing box is bolted directly to the hull or stern tube. The flexible type connects the stuffing box to the stern tube or cutless bearing by a short, flexible length of rubber hose double-clamped at both ends.

Another option

For those who find the constant drip of water into the bilge to be discon-certing, or for those who find it difficult or impossible to negotiate the con-tortions required to adjust the compression and lock nuts on the stuffing box, a dripless seal is the answer.

These dripless shaft seals replace the stuffing box and are a newer method of providing a seal that is completely watertight. A rubber bellows is used instead of the straight rubber hose, to connect the dripless seal to the stern tube or cutless bearing. At the forward end of this bellows is fas-tened a polished carbon flange, which is compressed by the bellows against a polished stainless-steel rotor attached to the shaft. Thus, the carbon flange remains fixed to the rubber bellows, while the stainless-steel rotor rotates with the shaft. The tolerances on this seal are so close that there is no drip, and heat from friction is reduced by the natural lubricating prop-erties of the carbon and the cooling water just behind the seal. This seal does not require the frequent, awkward readjustments that are required by

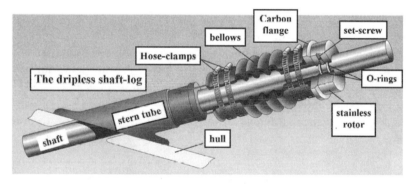

The basic parts of one type of dripless shaft-log,
in which the stainless steel rotor, which is attached to the shaft,
rotates against a carbon/graphite plate, which is attached
to the bellows and is non-rotating. The tolerances between
the two are so accurate that it is watertight.
The stern tube leads the propeller shaft through the hull to
either an external strut, which incorporates the cutless bearing,
or the stern tube will have a built-in cutless bearing.
Courtesy of Ted Tollefson

the conventional stuffing box, or the periodic removal of the old packing and its replacement. It also prevents the scoring of the propeller shaft that is a long-term problem with stuffing boxes.

The cutless bearing

The cutless bearing provides support and alignment for the propeller shaft. It is a bronze, stainless-steel, or fiberglass tube with a grooved nitrile-rubber or plastic liner inside. The propeller shaft is supported by this cutless bearing inside the stern tube or in an external strut and, when new, should allow little or no play in the propeller shaft. The groves in the liner allow outside cooling water to enter the cutless bearing for cooling both the propeller shaft and seal.

Signs that a cutless bearing needs replacement are vibration when in gear, and a propeller shaft that shows $\frac{1}{16}$ inch or more of play. Replacing a cutless bearing can be quite a task. Although the bearing itself is relatively inexpensive, the replacement process can be complicated and frustrating. It usually requires the removal of the propeller shaft, which, in turn, often means removal of the rudder. The set screws holding the cutless bearing to the stern tube are then removed, and a cutless-bearing puller is used to remove the old bearing. A new bearing can then be slid in place. If it's a tight fit, keeping it in the refrigerator or freezer overnight will usually shrink it enough to make the job easier. Then the greased propeller shaft can be slid into place, coupled to the engine, the propeller and rudder installed, and the engine's alignment checked.

A properly aligned cutless bearing should last for several thousand hours.

The Hull

The HIN—Your Boat's Birth Certificate

Unless you have a really old, old boat, you probably have a strange set of twelve characters imbedded on the upper, starboard side of the transom. This is your boat's birth certificate, the Hull Identification Number (HIN). It shows the parentage and date of birth of your vessel. This identification is similar to the 17-character automobile identification number that's on the lower left side of the car's dashboard, close to the windshield, the VIN (Vehicle Identification Number). All boats that were either manufactured or imported after November 1, 1972 are required, by law, to have a HIN and, just as you would have a duplicate of your own birth certificate, it's a good idea to record your HIN, or a rubbing of it, in your records.

In addition to manufactured boats, this regulation also applies to backyard boat builders, and even though they will be using the boat for their own use, with no thought of selling it, they must obtain the 12-character HIN number from their state's boating agency. In the case of a home-built boat, the first three characters in the HIN, which are the manufacturer's identification code, are composed of the 2-character state identification followed by Z, indicating a home-built boat. Thus, for a home-built boat in Minnesota, the first three characters in the HIN would be MNZ.

The 12-character HIN bears no relationship to your state's boat registration number—the number you have applied to the port and starboard sides of your bow (unless your boat is documented). By contrast, the HIN is federally mandated, and it is also required to be shown on the state's boat registration certificate.

The 1972 HIN formats

To read your boat's birth certificate you have to be able to decipher the format of those 12 characters on the stern. There have been several formats for the HIN over the years, and it's probable that new formats will emerge in the future. From its inception on November 1, 1972, the HIN was designated by one of the two following formats.

In these two formats, the manufacturer had a choice of using either the model year format or the straight year format, both of which identified the month and year of production.

Characters 1, 2, and 3 of the HIN are the manufacturer's identification code, which is assigned by the federal government.

1972 HIN "Straight Year" format:

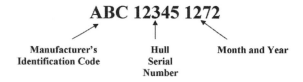

ABC 12345 1272

Manufacturer's
Identification Code

Hull
Serial
Number

Month and Year

1972 HIN "Model Year" format:

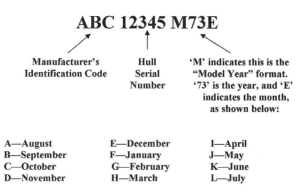

ABC 12345 M73E

Manufacturer's
Identification Code

Hull
Serial
Number

'M' indicates this is the
"Model Year" format.
'73' is the year, and 'E'
indicates the month,
as shown below:

A—August   E—December   I—April
B—September   F—January   J—May
C—October   G—February   K—June
D—November   H—March   L—July

Note: spaces shown in the examples above are only
for explanation purposes. There are no spaces in the HIN.

Characters 4 through 8 is the alpha-numeric serial number, assigned at the discretion of the manufacturer (I, O, or Q cannot be used in this serial number).

In the model year format, the ninth character will always be M, indicating the manufacturer is using the model year format; characters 10 and 11 indicate the year, and character 12 is a letter indicating a month, starting with August. Thus, if characters 9 through 12 of the HIN were "M80B," the boat was built in September of 1980. Why the lettering of the months in the model year system began with August is not known.

In the numerical straight year format, characters 9 through 12 are simply the month and year of production, thus, 0879 would indicate August 1979.

The 1984 format

Optional, as of January 1, 1984, was a new format version, simply called "New Format." This single new format became mandatory on August 1, 1984, replacing the two previous formats.

1984 HIN New Format:

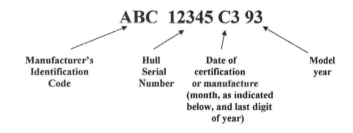

ABC 12345 C3 93

| Manufacturer's Identification Code | Hull Serial Number | Date of certification or manufacture (month, as indicated below, and last digit of year) | Model year |

A—January	E—May	I—September	
B—February	F—June	J—October	
C—March	G—July	K—November	
D—April	H—August	L—December	

Note: spaces shown in the examples above are only for explanation purposes. There are no spaces in the HIN.

In the New Format, you'll see that characters 1, 2, and 3 are still the manufacturer's identification code, which is assigned by the government. Sometimes the letters of this manufacturer's code easily identify the manufacturer. In other cases they bear no relationship to the manufacturer's name.

Characters 4 through 8 are still the alpha-numeric serial number, assigned at the discretion of the manufacturer. Some of these manufacturer-assigned characters are laid out very logically, and some defy logic. On a 37-footer, which is hull #51, the number might be 37051; but it also might be a set of characters that only makes sense to the builder.

Character 9 indicates the month of manufacture or certification. A designates January, B February, and so on, till December (a big improvement over the original lettering system that started in August).

Character 10 is a numeral that indicates the last digit of the year of manufacture or certification.

Characters 11 and 12 indicate the model year. Thus, "82" would indicate the boat's model year was 1982.

Some manufacturers also add additional information after the HIN, such as "-27," which might indicate that this is their 27-foot model.

In addition, after August 1, 1984, boat manufacturers were required to display two identical hull identification numbers, one on the outside starboard side of the transom, within two inches of the top of the transom, gunwale, or hull/deck joint—whichever is lowest. On boats where this is impossible—such as double-enders—the HIN must be on the starboard side of the hull, within one foot of the stern and within two inches from the top of the hull, gunwale, or deck joint.

The second HIN must be inside the hull in an unexposed location or beneath a fitting or item of hardware.

The HIN characters, both inside and outside the hull, must be no less than ¼" high, but many manufacturers make them much larger. It is illegal for anyone to alter or remove a HIN without written permission of the Commandant of the Coast Guard.

Although the HIN provides a great birth certificate for your boat, there are a few hitches in the system.

One problem is that foreign manufacturers might use a manufacturer's identification code (which is the first 3 characters of the HIN) that is not listed in the United States, or might even be the same as a U.S. manufacturer. Some United States builders have taken it on their own to add US to their HIN, to establish the country of origin and solve this problem.

It's obvious that the present 12-character HIN is becoming obsolete and outdated in the current global marketplace. For years the National Association of State Boating Law Administrators has been recommending that the HIN be increased to 17 characters—the same number of characters as your automobile's Vehicle Identification Number (VIN). This expanded HIN would allow additional important information, such as the country of origin, type of vessel, hull material, length of vessel, propulsion, and fuel type.

But for now, the 12-character HIN is our present system, and the preceding information should enable you to trace the lineage of either the boat you own or the boat you plan to buy—that is, till a new format comes along.

To decipher those first three letters of the HIN, the MIC, you can go to: http://www.uscgboating.org/recalls/mic_database.htm

This will give you the manufacturer's name, address and phone number, as well as the status of the company.

Fiberglass

The history of fiberglass

Composite construction in the United States began in the 1940s, during World War II, when a southern California company, Chemold, was contracted by the military to produce molded plastic hulls. It used an acetate resin with a cotton fabric as the reinforcing agent. After the war the tooling was sold to Wizard Boat Company, which produced a line of small outboard hulls for the recreational boating market. In 1946 the Wizard Company began using polyester resin and eventually switched to a reinforcing material made from glass fibers. In June of that year, the Winner Company, in Trenton, New Jersey, received a Navy contract to develop 28-foot motorboats from this new material. Those early boats were formed over a male mold. Sailboats were first produced by this new process in 1947, by the Glasspar Company.

The original polyester resin was a difficult material to use, and required a sunlight cure. Not surprisingly, many of the first companies to use this process made their homes in southern California. This curing process was soon replaced by curing the polyester resin with a catalyst mixed into the resin before application. This catalyst, methyl-ethyl-ketone-peroxide (MEKP), along with a cobalt accelerator that is usually pre-mixed in the resin, allows the builder a limited amount of layup time, depending on the amount and type of catalyst, and the ambient temperature.

It wasn't long before boatbuilders all around the world began using this new technique; but in the 1950s the word "plastic" was regarded with distrust, so manufacturers avoided that word in their advertising and "fiberglass" became the generic advertising term for this new product. Fiberglass-reinforced plastic, FRP, is a more proper name for this material (in Europe it is called GRP, glass-reinforced plastic).

184

Construction methods

Basic construction of a fiberglass hull uses a relatively low-strength resin, reinforced and made stronger with internal fibers of various types. The most common of these fibers is glass, although Kevlar and graphite fibers are also sometimes used. The plastic, mainly polymers, but sometimes epoxy or vinylesters, is usually of a thermosetting type. Thermosetting is the capability of a substance to become permanently rigid when heated. The thermal agitation of the molecules of the resin aids the chemical process that links the molecules together in a process called *polymerization*. There are wide variations in the formulations of these resins, depending on the specific requirements of the finished product.

Adding fibers to a building product to increase its strength is not a new concept; it goes back thousands of years. Early builders mixed straw into mud bricks, and much later steel reinforcing rods were added to concrete to increase the tensile strength of the composite.

A fiberglass hull usually takes its shape inside a female mold, onto which a special wax, with no affinity for the resin, is applied. This prevents the layup from sticking to the mold. A gelcoat is then applied, usually by spraying. This gelcoat is a special, thin, pigmented formulation, which contains no reinforcement. It is followed by alternate layers of fiberglass reinforcements, plastic resin, and sometimes core material, which are applied until the desired thickness and strength are obtained.

One of the first layers of glass reinforcing materials is often applied with a chopper gun, which sprays the resin and the catalyzer, in the proper proportions, while simultaneously cutting a loose bundle of continuous glass fiber strands, or rovings, into short pieces and projecting the composite mix into the mold. It has the advantage of easily filling the angles and corners in the mold and making the layup of subsequent layers easier. Since these glass fibers are in random orientation, strength is equal in all directions.

The bundles of fiberglass rovings used in the chopper gun can also be woven together at right angles into a coarse cloth, which has the appropriate name of woven roving; when laid at right angles and stitched together, it is known as stitch mat. These materials are the basis of most laminates; but since they have a coarse texture and relatively low strength, chopped stranded mat (CSM) is usually interspersed between layers.

Chopped stranded mat, commonly known as mat, consists of chopped fiberglass fibers, about two inches long, in random directions, that are compressed and loosely bound together into a mat with a binder that dissolves in the resin. Mat produces a layer similar to that of the chopper gun and is the most used material in fabricating boat hulls.

Fiberglass cloth is a fine and tightly woven fabric made from continuous glass fibers. It gives a nice smooth finish and was widely used in the early days, but because of its expense it is now seldom used except in places that demand a high strength-to-weight ratio. Cloth, woven roving, and stitch mat have strands at right angles, and are said to have bidirectional strength.

Unidirectional fabric consists of fibers that only run in one direction and are held together with a binder. These fabrics are used when strength in only one direction is required.

During hand layup the resin can be applied by brushing, troweling, rolling, or spraying. The resin penetrates the reinforcing fibers and, when cured, the result is a strong monolith.

Weight-saving stiffeners, or cores, are often incorporated in the layup, and can be materials such as plywood, end-grain balsa, or synthetic honeycomb.

Although fiberglass weighs about 106 pounds per cubic foot—about three times the weight of hardwood—it only needs to be about half the thickness of the hull of a wood boat, and will not require as many heavy frames; so the entire hull ends up weighing less than a wooden boat of similar size.

Soda Blasting

If you're the owner of an old boat, chances are that there are many years' worth of paint on the bottom. Removing those years of paint buildup without ruining the substrate—the wood, fiberglass gelcoat, aluminum, or steel—has always been a vexing problem. For years one of the old tried-and-true methods of stripping off these layers has been by sand-blasting. All blasting processes use pressurized air containing suspended particles that are projected on a surface for the purpose of removing a coating. But recently a new variation of abrasive blasting has become popular with boaters, soda blasting. Instead of sand, baking soda, or sodium bicarbonate ($NaHCO3$) is used as the abrasive material. Although seemingly a bit bizarre, the use of baking soda has many advantages over sand when removing bottom paint, especially on recreational boats.

Soda-blasting advantages

Sodium bicarbonate is a unique blasting medium because its crystals are sharp yet soft, and when they impact on a surface they fracture into smaller particles, which intensifies the cleaning action. Abrasive particles that act in this manner are termed friable. This friable characteristic is especially effective in getting rid of grease, dirt, and bottom paint, without substantially affecting the boat's hull. Of course, if the soda-blasting nozzle were left on one spot, gelcoat would eventually be worn through, so the operator's experience and technique are a factor. The soda-blasting process produces a cleaner surface than other processes currently being used. After the surface has been washed of residue and neutralized, it's ready to be painted, or for a barrier coat.

Baking soda is environmentally friendly. With a benign pH of 8.2, the soda itself is water-soluble, biodegradable, non-flammable, non-toxic, and not hazardous to the health of the worker. (The coating being removed, however, can be very toxic, which requires workers' safety requirements. Proper containment and waste disposal are also necessary).

The baking soda used for soda blasting is not your mother's kitchen variety. There are over a dozen formulations of abrasive sodas available, depending on the application. The differences are mainly in particle size and uniformity, as well as the added ingredients for flowability and rinsability. These soda particles are delivered under relatively low pressure but at a high velocity, that enables them to scour virtually any coating while softening the impact on the substrate.

The operation

The soda-blasting process begins with creating a tent around the boat, in which the operator works. On the ground inside this tent is a tarpaulin to collect the residue, primarily the bottom paint.

The operator, who is dressed in a hazardous-materials suit with facemask and respirator, begins the blasting, which can take several hours for the average sailboat with multiple layers of paint.

A tent is built around the bottom of the boat to contain
the toxic bottom-paint that is being removed

The soda-blasted hull is now ready for the
barrier coats and/or bottom paint

Water is used with the blasting process, to reduce the dust. After the soda blasting, the boat is hosed down. It is then washed with a low pH solution, which neutralizes the baking soda's higher pH. This is followed by hosing or power spraying off the neutralizer. When dry, the hull is ready for painting.

The cost of the procedure runs in the neighborhood of $16 per foot of waterline length plus the cost of each bag of baking soda that is used. The number of bags used will be determined by the numbers of layers and type of bottom paint that is being removed. For a boat with several years of accumulated paint, you might figure about a bag of soda for every 4-5 feet of waterline, at roughly $25 a bag.

Don't be surprised if your boat operates more sprightly when it's back in the water. For a boat with a decade or more of paint on the bottom, the weight of the paint removed can be in the hundreds of pounds. For powerboats, it's even more noticeable, with owners reporting that their boats get up on a plane at a much lower rpm than before.

Hatch Doors

One thing for sure about being aboard a boat is that the weather is never the same for very long. There are times when you don't need hatch doors at all, times when heavy-duty doors never seem strong enough, times when it's warm and balmy, but you need screens to keep the bugs out and times when it's pouring rain or chilly outside and you want to close up without feeling like you're in a cave.

After many years of cruising we have come up with a solution to the hatch-door problem that has proved very practical for us. Our solution is to have three sets of interchangeable cabin doors to meet all weather conditions.

Our hatch doors are on lift-off hinges, and the hinges, on all three pair of doors, are compatible, so that in a matter of seconds one pair of doors can be replaced by another pair. Since there are as many dimensions for drop-on hinges as there are manufacturers, to make the hinges interchangeable, sticking with the same manufacturer is a must.

Our main hatch doors are made of heavy 1½ inch teak, with a built-in lock and dead bolt. These strong doors are the ones we use when we're out in rough seas or for security when leaving our boat unattended.

For those hot summer days when the bugs are annoying, we have a pair of screen hatch doors with teak frames, that we can drop in place. Even though all eleven of our bronze ports open and have screens, and our forward hatch can open in either direction and has a screen, the added airflow with screened-in hatch doors makes a big difference. This is especially true when in a berth with the breeze coming from astern. These hatchway screen doors have the added advantages of letting in light as well as providing a view outside.

Lift-off hinges are used on all three sets of hatch doors

Once, while in a transient slip in Cape May, we had several days of cold, windy rain, pelting the cabin from our stern. We used our third pair of hatch doors to keep us dry and cozy inside while allowing the maximum amount of light in the cabin. This third pair of hatch doors is made of ¼ inch clear acrylic. Although they have the drop-on hinges of the other doors, they have no frames. They're wonderful for keeping out the rain and cold while maintaining the feel of an open hatch. We find these doors are also handy on sunny days during the off-seasons, not only keeping the cold out but also creating a nice greenhouse effect.

Our two sets of unused doors are stored in slip-covers made of Sunbrella, in a color that matches our dodger and sail covers. This rugged material protects the doors from scratches and keeps them paired together. Our two unused sets of doors are usually kept on a quarter berth, unless our granddaughters are sailing with us. Then we keep them in the lazarette—the hatch doors, that is, not the granddaughters.

Our normal
storm and
security
hatch doors

The screen
hatch doors

Clear acrylic
hatch doors

Shorepower Cable Protection

At our dock we have three shore cables: a 35-amp AC power cable; a telephone cable; and the TV cable. To keep the shore-end plugs of these cables out of the weather when they're are not being used, we've installed a short section of capped PVC pipe, of appropriate diameter, on the piling next to our shorepower pedestal, and we tuck the unused cable plugs up into this section of pipe. This keeps them dry and retards tarnishing of the prongs—which is accelerated when they are exposed to sun, rain, or snow. This tarnishing is most noticeable in the poor performance of the TV and telephone. Tarnishing of the AC power cord prongs can lead to a greater danger—severe overheating of the plug due to poor electrical contacts.

When the shorepower cables are not connected to the power pedestal on the left, the ends are tucked up inside the PVC pipe, behind the pedestal

In the Cabin

Cabin Heaters

Heating your boat in the off-seasons makes sailing more enjoyable and extends your time on the water. For any planned heater installation, three things must be considered: ventilation, insulation, and safety.

Moisture is constantly being produced in the cabin, from breathing, condensation, cooking, and open flames. This moist, warm air must be replaced with dry, cool, outside air, even though this seems to be counterproductive. Ventilation is necessary to reduce the moisture in the cabin and to maintain proper oxygen content in the cabin air.

Also, since any flame from either a stove or a cabin heater can be potentially lethal, a carbon monoxide monitor is mandatory. To reduce these negative by-products, a cabin heater that employs an open flame should always be vented.

Insulation is also important, not only for heat conservation, but also since a well-insulated boat will produce less condensation.

Using the engine's heat

While motoring, your engine is an excellent source of heat. Using an automobile-type heater with a blower (built to marine specifications) allows you to use the heated engine coolant to heat the cabin, just as with an automobile. These heaters are often marketed as *hydronic heaters*. When motoring on a cold day this "free" heat that is normally wasted helps make the cabin snug and cozy. Kits can be purchased for this conversion, which will also allow this heat to be ducted into separate cabins.

A typical heat-exchanger
installation kit for transferring
engine heat into cabin heat.
Courtesy of Ted Tollefson

A cabin grill-plate
which distributes heat
from the engine

Electric heat

If you are at a dock with adequate shorepower, an electric heater is very convenient. This can be either a portable heater, or a bulkhead-mounted recessed heater that is hard-wired into the boat's AC system. This is convenient at dock, but doesn't solve the problem when you're out on the water, unless you have a very large generator.

A bulkhead-
mounted, stainless
steel, electric cabin
heater, by BoatSafe

Unvented kerosene or propane floor heaters

Any unvented open flame in the cabin produces huge amounts of moisture and eats up oxygen, so this heating option requires a very large amount of ventilation (outside air). Coupled with the possibility of the heater could tip over, this choice is a poor one.

Bulkhead-mounted, vented LPG

A bulkhead-mounted, vented LPG cabin heater provides a high BTU output and a clean-burning flame, with the only electric drain being the LPG shut-off solenoid. As with all LPG installations, ABYC (American Boat and Yacht Council) specifications must be followed in the installation and operation, for safety reasons. All deck-vented installations require a "smokestack" on deck—a Charlie Noble. This usually requires a compromise between the ideal interior location for the cabin heater vis-à-vis the ideal deck location for the stack.

A kerosene, diesel, or propane cabin heater can also double as a small stove. The heater is normally mounted on a bulkhead, but in our schooner DELPHINUS, I have mounted it on the centerboard trunk

Bulkhead-mounted, vented kerosene or diesel

This is a common heating system aboard sailboats. It requires no electricity, the moisture it creates is vented outside, it burns easily-available fuel, and is not complicated to maintain or repair; however pre-heating is necessary when lighting the burner. On sailboats, the deck location for the stack is very important. It must be in a location that doesn't interfere with deck work and yet, at the same time, is not subject to backdrafts from a dodger or other deck gear.

Ducted, gasoline/kerosene/diesel/LPG forced-air heaters

A ducted, force-air heater has the advantage of being able to supply heat to several cabins. It does not use the cabin air for combustion, but is otherwise very similar to a home's oil-burner furnace. Since this type of heater requires a powerful fan, a fuel pump, as well as a glow plug for ignition, this installation has a relatively high current drain. This type of heater is available for gasoline, kerosene, diesel, or LPG fuel.

Diesel ranges

Diesel cooking stoves are seldom seen on recreational sailboats, except on large boats operating in very cold climates, where they also double as cabin heaters. Diesel stoves, which are usually quite heavy, provide a very hot flame and, in a boat with a diesel engine, the fuel can be supplied from the engine's fuel tanks. Pre-heating the burner is necessary, and diesel stoves must be vented through a stack on deck, where the precautions of interfering with deck work and possible backdrafts must be contended with.

Fireplaces/stoves

This type of small, vented fireplace burns solid fuel in the form of charcoal briquettes, coal, or wood. Although they have a special charm, they are seldom seen on today's boats due to the disadvantages of storing the fuel supply, constant tending, the cleaning and disposal of ashes, and the vented smoke that can stain the cabintop, sailcovers, and sails.

Alcohol heaters

These self-standing heaters are non-pressurized, rustproof heaters that require no priming. Instead, an absorbent material is saturated with the alcohol fuel (which helps prevent spills). This type of heater can also double as a single-burner stove. The downside is the alcohol aroma and the high price of the heating fuel.

Aladdin lamp

The kerosene Aladdin lamp, which uses a fragile mantle, produces a bright light as well as a large amount of heat. In the evening, when both light and heat are required, very often the Aladdin lamp will supply both needs. Of course ventilation is required for this unvented flame, and heat is not available without the associated bright light.

12V DC heaters

These heaters plug into a cigarette lighter socket. They usually draw a maximum of about 13 amps (most cigarette lighter sockets are fused at 15 amps) and produce a moderate heat of about 150 watts. Naturally, with a constant 13-amp drain, the boat's battery must be recharged frequently. About 300-400 BTU can be expected from 12V DC heaters.

Engine-compartment heaters

Marine engine compartment heaters are designed to turn on at about 45-degrees to keep the engine compartment above freezing. The *BoatSafe* units come in either 250 or 750 watt models and are made of moisture-resistant materials.

Galley Stoves

The selection of the best galley stove for use aboard your sailboat depends on the size of the boat, the layout of the galley, and the type and amount of cooking you plan to do. This selection also depends on your budget, with galley stoves running from $40 to $4,000.

There is a great variety of galley stoves and fuels: non-pressurized alcohol; pressurized alcohol; small liquefied propane or butane canisters; liquefied propane using large pressure tanks; compressed natural gas; kerosene; diesel; electric and ceramic-glass electric; and microwave.

Galley stoves are also available as combinations, such as an alcohol/electric combo, or an electric burner/microwave-oven combination.

These stoves come as a simple single-burner or as multi-burners with oven. A galley stove that is gimbaled has a distinct advantage and is usually mounted facing athwartships, so that level cooking can be done when the sailboat is heeled. Gimbaled stoves should also have a method for *preventing* the stove from gimbaling—usually a barrel-bolt. The pivots for a gimbaled stove should be as high as possible, and fiddles, around the edge of the stove-top, with adjustable arms that encircle the pots, should be high enough to prevent pots from moving. Galley stoves should obviously be corrosion-resistant, preferably stainless steel.

Liquefied Petroleum Gas (LPG)

Every year more and more boatowners are selecting LPG for their galley stoves, since these operate much like a home stove, and the LPG burner gives about twice the heat of alcohol. LPG can be butane, propane, or a mixture of the two. These gases become liquid under pressure and must be contained in specially designed tanks, with aluminum the preferred tank material. When pressure is released, the liquid becomes a gas, which burns hot and clean, but is very explosive. Both butane and propane are heavier than air, which means that the gas can collect in the bilge, so the strict safety protocols established by the American Boat and Yacht Council (ABYC) must be observed in the installation and operation of a LPG stove. Gas detectors, or "sniffers," should be part of the installation. LPG is available worldwide, however outside the US metric adapter fittings are necessary for refilling a tank that has American threads. Small, camping-style LPG stoves are available that use small fuel canisters that are discarded after use. These canisters are usually available in hardware or camping stores, but they should be treated just like the large tanks used for LPG and, when not in use, must not be stored belowdecks.

Alcohol

Other than the small, camping-stove type canister LPG stoves, alcohol stoves are the most inexpensive type of galley stove available, but they have about half the heat output of propane and butane. Alcohol vapor is heavier than air, and alcohol, which was once proclaimed as the safest of fuels, is now also considered dangerous when improperly or casually used. Non-pressurized alcohol stoves—those that contain a material saturated with alcohol and operate much like a Sterno stove—are much safer than the pressurized alcohol models. These non-pressurized stoves require no preheating which, with alcohol, can sometimes be a hazardous operation. The pressure for pressurized alcohol stoves comes from a tank that has to be pumped up with air and is either separate or integral to the stove. Alcohol is expensive in the US and very expensive and difficult to obtain elsewhere in the world.

Compressed Natural Gas (CNG)

The main advantage of CNG fuel (primarily methane) is safety, since it is lighter than air and will not accumulate in the bilge. Nevertheless, one should apply the safety standards of LPG to CNG. The tanks should not be stored in the cabin, although many installations ignore this admonition. Just as with LPG, the ABYC recommendations should be followed in the installation. These tanks are leased, not purchased as with a LPG tank, and when refueling, the empty tank is exchanged for a full one. CNG is more difficult to obtain than LPG and has a higher cost, mostly due to a more limited distribution infrastructure. CNG has lower BTUs-per-pound than LPG, and in any installation, a CNG tank cannot be substituted for LPG or vice versa.

Kerosene

Except for some older boats, kerosene galley stoves are seldom seen anymore. Kerosene is universally available and relatively inexpensive. Pressurized kerosene stoves burn kerosene vapor, and have a blue flame similar to an LPG stove. Just as with pressurized alcohol stoves, the burners must be pre-heated with alcohol to initialize the vaporization of the kerosene before use. The pressure for kerosene stoves comes from a pressure tank that has to be pumped up with air or, rarely, from an overhead tank that uses a gravity feed.

Electricity

Only sailboats with very high-output generators will have enough power to operate an all-electric galley since the power can be in the multiple thousands of watts. On small sailboats, a single-burner electric hotplate can be useful when in a marina and connected to adequate shorepower. For the ultimate in electric cooking tops, ceramic-glass electric galley stoves are also available, as well as 12 volt DC or 120 volt AC microwave ovens.

Diesel

Diesel stoves are seldom seen on recreational sailboats, except on large boats operating in very cold climates, where they double as cabin heaters. Diesel stoves, which are usually quite heavy, provide a very hot flame and, in a boat with a diesel engine, the fuel can be supplied from the engine's fuel tanks. Often the fuel is pumped from the engine's tanks into a small overhead tank, using a gravity feed to the stove. Pre-heating the burner is necessary, and diesel stoves must be vented through a Charlie Noble on deck.

Porthole Gutters

We have eleven bronze ports on our boat. We love them, and wouldn't think of changing them for the plastic variety. They are built to last a lifetime, and will certainly last longer than we will. They do have one disadvantage however, when days are warm and humid and the nights are cold, condensation collects on the interior of these bronze ports. Nothing is more jarring in the middle of the night than to have a cold drop of water fall on your face. To prevent this Chinese water torture we've installed small, teak gutters under each port and any condensation ends up dripping into the gutter. (We've also discovered that these gutters are just the right size to hold that chapstick that we are always misplacing).

These gutters, just above our V-berth, prevent condensation drip

Adjustable Dorade Vent

Dorade vents are great. They supply water-free air belowdecks even in a pouring rain or when spray is soaking the deck while beating to windward. We have two dorades on deck, one above the head and the other over the settee in the cabin. In the off-seasons, when we're sitting at the cabin table and a cold wind is blowing outside, the airflow from the dorade can cause a draft on the back of our necks. To solve this problem we have installed small sliding doors on the overhead under each of the dorade vents. This allows us to temporarily close off, or reduce, the air supply when we find it annoying, without having to go out on deck.

Our dorade vent with
the sliding door closed

The normally open
dorade vent

The Environment

Our Magnetic Earth

The Compass

Around 1090 AD the Chinese first documented the use of a magnetic needle to indicate north. This primitive compass was an iron needle, magnetized by a lodestone, inserted into a straw, and floating in a bowl of water. In Europe, the discovery of the magnetic compass didn't occur till over a century later, in the early 1200s, and historians don't know whether this European discovery was independent or whether it came to them from the East. The compass finally allowed the 13th-century European mariners to determine direction, even under overcast skies or during stormy weather. It was such a simple device, with only one moving part, that it seemed like magic. Many captains were afraid to use it. It was the age of the Inquisition, and sailors feared that if they were seen using this device, they could be accused of witchcraft, which could result in torture and death. It wasn't till nearly a century later, during the 1300s, when seamen could finally use the compass openly and without fear.

For the next 100 years mariners believed that the compass pointed to true north, but during the 1400s scientists determined that there was a difference between compass north and true north. Finally, in the 1590s, the Portuguese developed surprisingly accurate tables that showed the differences between true and magnetic north (variation) at various places on the globe.

In the 1600s, it was discovered that the magnetic poles changed location from year to year and that the intensity of the magnetic field also varied. Our concepts of a simple magnetic planet were beginning to change.

Magnets

There are basically two types of magnets, a simple bar magnet, and electro-magnets created by the flow of electricity.

In nearly all representations of the Earth's magnetic field, the Earth's magnet is represented as a simple bar magnet. In reality, the Earth's magnetism is more closely related to that of an electromagnet.

The Earth's magnetic field is created in the molten iron in the Earth's outer core, about 1,850 miles below the Earth's surface. The Earth's magnetic field is produced by electrical currents that originate in this hot, liquid, outer core of the Earth, which is moving around the solid inner core and acting like a huge electromagnet.

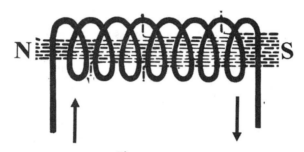

Electromagnet

Wandering poles

The magnetic north pole has been wandering around the polar regions for millions of years. By using data from the 1500s to the present, we see that during this relatively brief period in the history of the Earth, the magnetic north pole has made a trip from the Arctic Ocean into northern Canada north of Hudson Bay, and is now on its way back to the Arctic Ocean at an average speed of about 10 to 15 miles per year. But it is almost impossible to predict where the magnetic pole will go. As Larry Newitt of the Geological Survey of Canada says, "Although it has been moving north or northwest for a hundred years, it is not going to continue in that direction forever. Its speed has increased considerably during the past 25 years, and it could just as easily decrease a few years from now."

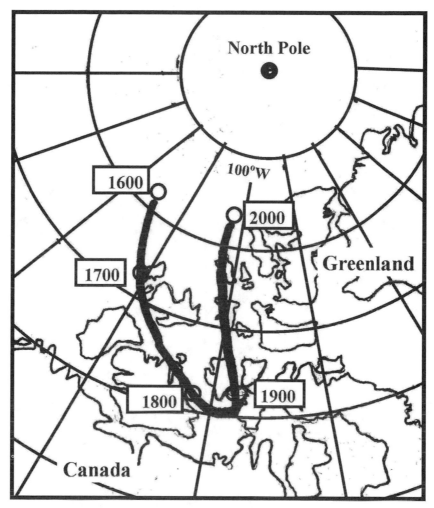

The movement of the Earth's magnetic pole
over the last four centuries

In addition to the long-term movement of the magnetic poles, there is also a daily (diurnal) movement of the poles. This daily movement of the poles roughly follows an elliptical path around the pole's average position. Sometimes this daily movement follows the path of a very small ellipse, and sometimes a very large one. This can cause the pole to move over 100 miles during a 24-hour period. It's believed that this diurnal movement is caused

211

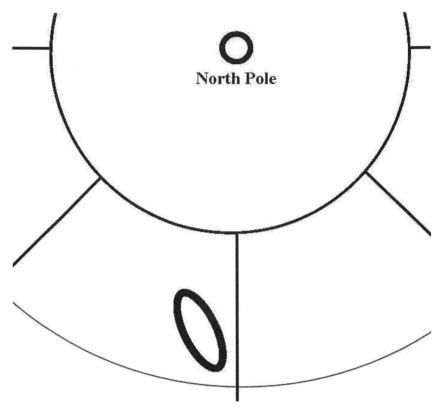

The daily (diurnal) movement of the Earth's magnetic pole
follows a rough ellipse with variations in size and shape

by the solar wind, and that solar storms on the surface of the sun can cause
a change in the size and shape of this elliptic path.

To make things even more confusing, most scientific organizations,
such as the *American Geophysical Union*, consider the term "magnetic pole"
to be an oversimplified representation, and prefer to describe at least three
different sets of poles, with the International Geomagnetic Reference Field
(IGRF) Model Dip Pole as the closest to what most cartographers, and the
public in general, refer to as the magnetic pole.

Variation and isogonic lines

The difference in angle between magnetic north and true north is called *variation* by mariners. In the scientific community this difference is often called *magnetic declination* or *deviation*. This is unfortunate since, for the sailor, deviation means something quite different.

Although the magnetic lines of force shown around simple magnets are smooth and regular, the magnetic lines of force around the Earth are extremely irregular, primarily due to the non-uniform distribution of magnetic material within the Earth. Those erratic lines that show the same variation are known as isogonic lines, and maps are available which show these lines worldwide. But these large-scale maps don't show the many small irregularities existing locally which, in many cases, can be enormous. Off the Australian coast, for example, there is a position where, in the distance of two football fields, the compass changes by 90 degrees.

Reversing magnetism

There is another bizarre event that occurs with the magnetic poles. About every 250,000 years the poles reverse themselves—the north pole becomes the south pole and vice versa. During the last 5 million years this has happened about 25 times. But it has been 780,000 years since this happened the last time, and a reversal is long overdue. However, since the timing of this reversal has always been erratic, it's impossible to tell when it will happen again. Nevertheless, the planet's magnetic field is showing signs of wanting to make the gigantic switch once more. The prelude to this changeover is the gradual weakening of the Earth's magnetic field till it becomes zero. Results from measuring the Earth's magnetic field in 1980 by the Magsat satellite, and in 2000 from the Orsted satellite, show a reduction in strength is in progress. When the Earth finally becomes non-magnetic, it will remain that way for possibly several hundred years. Then the magnetism will begin to build up in the opposite direction. For the last 4000 years, this weakening has continued to progress. Just in the past century, the strength of the magnetic field has decreased 5%, and scientists predict the Earth's magnetic field will cease to exist in several hundred to a few thousand years—just an instant in geological time.

During the time when the Earth is non-magnetic, compasses, which will point nowhere in particular, will be relegated to museums and children will ask their parents, in awe, "Was the Earth once really a magnet?" It's also probable that harmful radiation levels reaching the surface of the earth will increase during this period, when the protection of the magnetic field surrounding the Earth has vanished.

Debate has raged among scientists for over 150 years as to how birds, bees, frogs, spiny lobsters, and other creatures are able to consistently and unerringly navigate from one place to another. The latest theory is based on the discovery of a naturally iron-rich substance in their brains, called biogenic magnetite, which can detect magnetic fields.

Perhaps the many centuries it will take for the earth to lose its magnet-ism will give those migratory animals, who navigate using the Earth's magnetic field, a new way to locate their seasonal destinations.

Although it can be intimidating to reflect on all the changes that are taking place in our magnetic Earth, don't throw away your compasses yet! In our lifetime it will still remain as our basic tool for non-electronic navigation.

For further information on our magnetic Earth, see *The Compass*, in the *Navigation* section of this book.

Tides

Poets and ancient cultures have long compared life itself with the tides. Historically, a flood tide has been considered an omen of good fortune, and an ebb tide has been looked at with foreboding. Dickens wrote, "He's a-going out with the tide." In fact along the North Sea coast of England it was believed that most deaths occurred at ebb tide. In 77 AD Pliny described tides in his *Natural History*, but it wasn't until Sir Isaac Newton presented his theory of gravitation in his book *Principia*, one of the greatest scientific works, that this phenomenon was explained more fully.

The earliest known tidetable was compiled by the monks of St. Albans, near London, in the thirteenth century. It predicted the tides for each day of the Moon's age for the waters at London Bridge. This tidetable, or "rutter," copied by hand, was made available to the mariners who navigated the Thames.

Celestial tides

Now, tides are no longer completely wrapped in mystery. They are created chiefly from the gravitational effects of the Moon and the Sun, as well as from atmospheric pressure and wind. Even though the Sun's mass is 26 million times that of the Moon, the Moon is 400 times closer, so it is the major force in creating tides; because of its closeness its gravitational pull is over two times that of the Sun, so that our tides usually follow the Moon, but are slightly modified by the gravitation of the Sun.

In most parts of the world the gravitational effects of the Moon and the Sun create two high and two low tides every day (or, to be little more accurate, every 24 hours and fifty minutes), these are *semidiurnal* tides. One of these semidiurnal high tides each day is when the Moon is overhead

215

and the other is when the Moon is on the opposite side of the Earth. There are a few places on Earth, such as parts of the Gulf of Mexico, where there is only one tide change each day, due to local coastal and bathymetric configurations. These are *diurnal* tides. *Mixed* tides ("diurnal inequality") are an amalgam of the two, where one is usually stronger than the other.

Accompanying these vertical rises and falls of water are various complex lateral movements, known as *tidal currents*. A current flowing toward shore or upstream is called a flood current; and one flowing away from land, or downstream, is an ebb current. During the period of reversal between flood and ebb, we have slack water.

The Moon rotates around the Earth so that it passes over the same longitude about once every 24 hours, 50 minutes and 28 seconds. This means that at any given location, celestial tides, that is, those created by the Moon and Sun, occur fifty minutes and 28 seconds later every day. If you see high tide at 9 a.m. Monday morning, you can expect a high tide to occur about 9:50 a.m. Tuesday morning, at about 10:40 a.m. Wednesday morning, and so forth. Due to several variables, such as the shape of continents and estuaries; the depths of the sea beds; the frictional drag between the water and the Earth; the Coriolis effect; and the changes in the Moon's orbital plane, the difference in time from when the Moon passes a certain point's longitude and when that point experiences high tide is called the *high-water interval*. The *low-water interval* is the time difference from the Moon's meridian crossing till the next low tide.

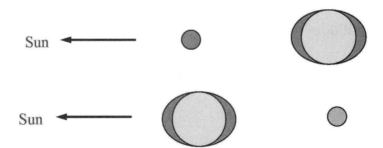

Spring Tides are produced when the Sun and the Moon
are in line, creating the greatest pull on the ocean's waters.
Spring Tides, which occur during the times of the *full moon*
(bottom) or *new moon* (top), generate the largest range
between high and low in the monthly cycle

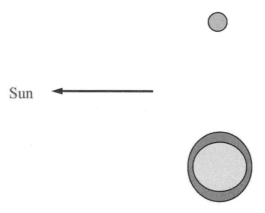

Sun ←————————

Neap Tides occur when the Moon is in its *first quarter*
or *last quarter,* and produces smaller ranges of tides since
the Sun and the Moon are attracting the Earth's waters
at right angles to each other

When the Sun and the Moon are in line with the Earth, which happens at the time of a new moon or a full moon, the gravitational pull is greater than average, and so-called *spring* tides occur. In this case, *spring* does not refer to the time of year but rather the welling-up of the water, as from a spring.

When the Sun and the Moon are at right angles to the Earth, with the Moon in its first or third quarter, the gravitational pulls of the Moon and Sun tend to cancel out slightly, and we have less than average, or *neap* tides. Near the times of the equinoxes (March 21 and September 22), the spring tides are usually larger, and near the time of the solstices (June 21 and December 22), spring tides are usually smaller than normal.

Other causes of tide variation

The Moon's orbit around the Earth is not circular but, like all other heavenly bodies, elliptical. So the Moon's gravitation is stronger at its *Perigee* (when closest to the Earth) than at its *Apogee* (farthest from the Earth).

Also, the Moon's orbit around the Earth is inclined in relation to the equator. Its declination is over the southern hemisphere part of the time and over the northern hemisphere part of the time, and only directly over the equator twice a month, at which time the two daily high tides will be about the same height. When north or south of the equator, these daily tide heights will be different (semidiurnal inequality).

217

Orbital tides

The Earth and Moon travel around the Sun as a single, combined mass. Visualize, if you will, a barbell, with a heavy weight on one end of the bar (the Earth) and a small weight on the other end of the bar (the Moon). The bar connecting the two represents the gravitational attractions of the Earth and Moon. Now, if we go to pick up the barbell with one hand, we will have to do it with our hand on the bar very close to the heavier weight to keep it in balance. This position is the center of mass of the barbell's heavy and small weight combination. If we were able to fling the barbell through the air in a rotating motion, we would find that it is this center of mass that follows a smooth trajectory, while the heavy and the light ends of the barbell rotate back and forth across this smooth trajectory—rotating around the center of mass.

The same holds true for the Earth/Moon combination. It is the center of mass that rotates in a relatively smooth orbit around the Sun. Thus, since the Earth and Moon are rotating around this center of mass, it means that both the Moon and, to a lesser extent the Earth, swing inside and outside of the orbit. So instead of the Earth rotating around the Sun in a nice, neat ellipse, as we like to think, it actually swings inside and outside this ellipse with the phases of the Moon.

Now visualize a car going down the center line of a highway. If that car swerves back and forth across the center line, the passengers will be thrown from one side to the other by centrifugal force. This same centrifugal force throws the water back and forth across the face of the Earth as the Earth swerves back and forth across the smooth orbit—adding an additional factor into our previously simple tidal concepts.

Intracoastal variations

Intracoastal tides (those tides occurring inland of the coastline) become even more complex. The mainland of the East and Gulf coasts, from New York to the Mexican border, is protected by barrier islands, broken intermittently by narrow inlets to the sea. Inside these barrier islands, on intracoastal waters, the tides are considerably less than those on the ocean side of the barrier islands. This is because the narrow inlets limit the exchanged of water between the ocean and the intracoastal bays, rivers, and sounds. This limited water exchange causes low tides on the inland bays that are higher than low tides in the ocean, and high tides lower than the ocean high

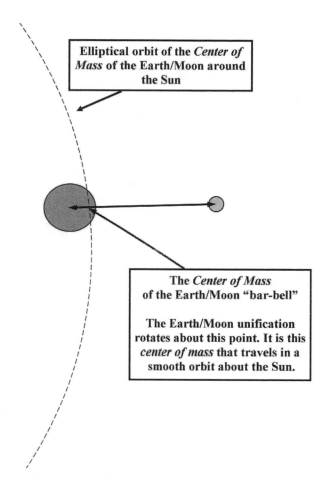

Elliptical orbit of the *Center of Mass* of the Earth/Moon around the Sun

The *Center of Mass* of the Earth/Moon "bar-bell"

The Earth/Moon unification rotates about this point. It is this *center of mass* that travels in a smooth orbit about the Sun.

tides. The reason for this is that at high tide the ocean tries to fill up the inland bays through the narrow inlets, but before it gets a chance, the tide has changed and begun to drop. The same thing happens at low tide when the water rushes out of the bays but the ocean tide changes before this can happen completely. Hence, the tide variations in these intracoastal waters never approach those on the ocean side of the islands. But as an ocean high tide starts decreasing, it is still higher than the waters in the back bays, and water keeps flowing into these bays. Thus, the times of high tides in intracoastal waters lag behind those for the ocean. The same scenario also holds true for low tides.

Atmospheric tides

The tides created by the gravitation of the Moon and Sun are known as celestial tides, as opposed to those tidal effects created by atmospheric pressure or the wind. Printed tide tables, as well as tide computer programs, allow the celestial tides to be calculated years in advance. One of the things these tables and programs can't show us, however, is the effect of atmospheric pressure and wind on the tides—and both of these influences are of great importance to the boaters and residents of coastal areas.

Storms, hurricanes, and nor'easters pose special problems along coastal shores. During an extended blow an added scenario takes place. During a long blow (twelve hours or more) an ocean current is produced by the wind. The rule of thumb is that this current is about two percent of the wind speed, so that during an extended blow of 60 mph toward a shore, a current of 1.2 mph is set up. When this current is directed toward the coastline it causes the water to mound up against the shore, creating higher than predicted tides. This effect is very real, with the ocean water level along the shore much higher than it is many miles out to sea. On top of this water are the unusually high wind-created waves. The height of these waves is directly related to the wind speed, its duration, and the distance that these winds are blowing across the water, or the *fetch*.

This mounding up of the water along the coastline during a storm, created by the winds and the current, forces the ocean waters into the inlets between barrier islands. Even during celestial low tide, the height of the ocean water, along with the wind, does not allow water to escape from the bays. The next ocean high tide again adds water to the bays until, after a series of high tides, the water level in the bays approaches that of high tide in the ocean.

Also, in a hurricane or nor'easter, the low pressure in the eye can suck up the ocean into unusually high tides. The combination of the mounding up of water along a coast due to the wind and the additional increase in height due to the water being sucked up into the low-pressure eye is known as the *storm surge*. This storm surge is often more devastating than the damage caused by the wind.

But these wind-produced tides don't only affect ocean waters. Windy conditions can also dramatically affect large bodies of inland waters, such as the Great Lakes. In October 2001 a prolonged southwest wind of 30-50 mph, blowing across Lake Erie, dropped the water level at the west end of the lake by about five feet, while the water at the eastern end of the lake was raised by the same amount. Records show that on Lake Erie there has been up to an eleven-foot difference between the lake levels at Buffalo and Toledo, caused by the wind.

Finally, celestial tides don't only affect water. The Earth's crust also rises and falls in response to the gravitational effects of the Moon and Sun.

There are several terms used to describe our tides and how their levels are transposed into our nautical charts:

MHHW *Mean Higher High Water* is the high water level to which all bridge clearances are referenced and charted. In most parts of the world (except for a few places such as portions of the Gulf of Mexico) there are two high and two low tides each day. The Moon is the primary influence on the tides, and since the Moon's orbital plane around the Earth is canted in relation to the equator, one of the two daily highs is higher than the other. If we take the average, or mean, of only the higher of the two daily highs over a period of 19 years, we have the *Mean Higher High Water*. (Note: The 19-year period is called a Tidal Epoch, during which time every possible combination of the positions of the Earth, Sun, and Moon occurs.)

MHW *Mean High Water* is the mean, or average, of high waters taken over a 19-year period at a particular location.

MSL *Mean Sea Level* is a designation used in areas where there is no appreciable tidal range.

MLW *Mean Low Water* is the average level of low tides that occur in a specific location over a 19-year period of time.

MLLW *Mean Lower Low Water*. If we take the average, or mean, of only the lower of the two daily lows over a period of 19 years, we have the *Mean Lower Low Water*. The term *Mean Lower Low Water* is frequently used in NOAA weather forecasts, and in the U.S. it is used as the reference for depth soundings on charts.

As we learn more about the tides, we discover that our studies lead us further and further into more complex concepts—and for sailors, the understanding of these concepts not only contributes to our safety on the water but also contributes to the sense of our tiny place in the universe.

Shipworms

Since the 1976 Federal Clean Waters Act, the resultant reduced pollution has meant a resurgence of marine life, including marine borers that feed on bulkheads, wharves, docks, and wooden boats. The irony of having cleaner waters is that all wood in contact with the water is now being attacked at an alarming rate. Huck DeVenzio, of Hickson Corporation, a supplier of treated lumber, says, "When waterways were badly polluted, substandard treated wood could last a deceptively long time—there weren't many wood-destroying organisms living in the polluted water. As water was cleaned up, the lack of proper wood treatment became more obvious; wood-destroying organisms became more prevalent, and insufficiently protected wood didn't last long."

Return of the marine life

Until fifty years ago professional mariners termed New York Harbor a "clean port," not because of the water purity, but because shipworms and isopods, which destroy wooden ships, barges and pilings, were unable to live in the polluted waters. As long as the waters remained polluted, the wooden boats and piers were spared. At that time manufacturing plants along the banks of the Hudson River and New York Harbor dumped waste chemicals into the water and the city disposed of more than 300 million gallons of raw sewage a day into the river and harbor. Finally public awareness of the problems caused activism to replace complacency, and the federal, state, and city governments were prompted by citizen groups to adopt stringent environmental regulations. Now, with the waters of New York Harbor cleaner than they have been in over 75 years, wood-eating organisms such as shipworms and gribbles (limnoria) are returning with a vengeance. Marine life is proliferating, even the species we would rather do without.

The return of shipworms to New York Harbor is particularly costly. The Port Authority is currently engaged in multi-million dollar projects for damage control. One approach is wrapping the pilings of two Brooklyn piers with plastic. Another involves reinforcing pilings near the Holland Tunnel with concrete. In addition, New York's Department of Transportation has spent millions of dollars for underwater surveys of the pilings that support the Franklin D. Roosevelt and Harlem River Drives, along the east side of Manhattan Island, and will be spending millions more for repairs.

New Jersey Transit will be forced to replace infested pilings at the Hoboken Ferry Terminal with concrete-filled steel pilings, a $79-million project. In Edgewater, NJ, the shipworms have created a multimillion dollar lawsuit by owners of the luxury Harbor Condominiums, which extend over the water on shipworm-infested pilings that were once used for a Ford Motor Company pier in the 1920s. Hartz Mountain Industries, the developer, claims that the lower salinity at their site will limit the amount of shipworm damage, and the present damage does not threaten the safety of the condominiums.

Environmentalists are delighted with the return of shipworms to New York Harbor and other coastal waters since it is an indication that these waters are becoming healthy again.

As with most marine life forms, proliferation of wood-eating organisms is cyclical, and can depend on water quality, salinity, predators and other wide-ranging influences. These cycles are most pronounced in estuaries and bays, where these cyclic variations are much more dramatic than in the open ocean.

The shipworm is not new

When all boats and ships were made of wood, the shipworm was a scourge that could result in your ship literally sinking from under you. Frequently crews had to abandon their craft because it was too rotten to sail any farther. In 1502, during the fourth voyage of Columbus to the Caribbean, his ships survived a hurricane, lightning, water spouts, and coral reefs, but two of the four ships had to be abandoned because of shipworm infestation.

The shipworm's attack scheme

But what are these little critters that can cause us so much grief? The shipworm is not a worm at all, but rather a highly specialized mollusk, or clam. Its shell is greatly reduced in size and is modified into a rasp for grinding the wood that provides the cellulose for its unique diet. When it is in its microscopic larval stage, the shipworm, which only lives in salt water, invades new wood. At this stage it is free-swimming, and its initial entrance hole into wood may be so tiny it's hard to detect. Creosote, a distillate of coal tar, and the oldest and most widely known preservative and deterrent, has been used for treating wood. More recently chemically-treated wood is now the product of choice. This treated wood, which comes in varying degrees of chemical saturation, offers good protection till, after a couple of decades, the active ingredient has disappeared.

Once inside edible wood the shipworm begins eating and growing. Some species can attain a length of over three feet. Since the shipworm remains in the interior of the wood structure, its body is protected from predators and the first hint of problems comes after the interior of the wood is nearly completely devoured and the outside wooden shell of the piling, bulkhead, or boat-planking disintegrates. This is the same attack plan as the land-based termite, so it's not surprising that the shipworm has been called the termite of the sea.

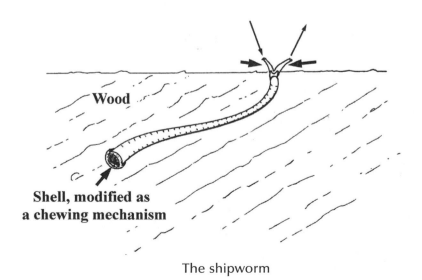

Wood

Shell, modified as
a chewing mechanism

The shipworm

The gribble

Another destroyer of wood is the gribble (limnoria). This tiny saltwater isopod often attacks the surface of wood. You may have seen pilings with a reduced diameter in one location, in an hourglass-type configuration. You can blame this on an infestation of the eighth-inch long gribbles, which usually confine themselves to one particular place on a piling.

Most bulkheads that have been destroyed are now being replaced with vinyl material. Although more expensive than either creosoted or chemically-saturated wood, it provides the dual advantages of an extended life—probably about 50 years—and a minimal impact on the immediate aquatic environment.

But as much as we complain about these wood-eating critters, our relationship with them isn't all bad. These same animals that can give us so much grief are also responsible for eliminating trees and branches that are washed down into our navigable waterways during storms, providing a natural clean-up system.

Sea Nettles

For years the jellyfish has been the bane of swimmers in the central Chesapeake Bay area. The popular name of this jellyfish is the sea nettle, which is appropriate, since its sting feels like those we've encountered when touching nettles. The bell-shaped body of the sea nettle has long tentacles suspended beneath it. These tentacles can reach five feet in length and they are armed with thousands of microscopic harpoons, called nematocysts. These harpoons are fired when a foreign object touches the nematocyst's trigger, and a paralyzing toxin is pumped up through the harpoon into the prey. Once paralyzed, the tentacles move the prey up into the mouth for digestion.

For swimmers, a single sting is very painful but usually not life-threatening; however multiple stings when in a cluster of sea nettles can prove to be very serious, and can even incapacitate an adult swimmer. Sea nettles have a limited swimming ability, but they can move both horizontally and vertically through the water by contracting the muscles in their bell-shaped bodies. This vertical movement is particularly hazardous to swimmers, since even though no sea nettles are seen on the surface, they may be hunting for prey below the surface. The color of sea nettles can vary between white and maroon, and some have a bluish color.

Where they occur

Sea nettles have always existed in temperate and tropical waters, and exist in waters all around the world. On the East Coast of the United States they are seen from Cape Cod on south, but large infestations, such as those in some of the waters of the Chesapeake have been relative rare.

New Jersey boaters have been smug about condemning and avoiding the summer waters of the Chesapeake Bay—until recently, when sea nettles

226

began multiplying in some sections of Barnegat Bay and other intracoastal waters at an alarming rate. Since the sea nettle survives and reproduces best in warm water of low salinity, outbreaks usually occur on inland waters well away from inlets, where fresh water streams or rain run-off lowers the salinity to the range they like—about 10 to 20 parts-per-thousand (ppt). Open ocean water in the northeast is generally in the 31 to 35 ppt range.

The sea nettle's diet is primarily the ctenophore, a tiny jellyfish—although it will occasionally sting, paralyze, and devour small minnows and other small aquatic prey. The ctenophore's diet, in turn, consists of tiny plants called phytoplankton. Phytoplankton, just like plants on land, grow best when nutrients, such as nitrogen and phosphorous are available. So, for sea nettles to multiply, they need brackish water and the nutrients for the food chain that creates their food source. In bays such as the Chesapeake Bay, brackish waters are found away from the mouth of the bay, especially to the north and west, where fresh water streams reduce the salinity to that preferred by the sea nettles. The other requirement, nutrients, is one which environmentalists have been warning against for decades—"non-point-source" pollution—that is, not from any specific one source, but from the watershed at large. These nutrients may come as agricultural run-offs from farms, but a large percentage of the nutrients that enter the intracoastal waters are from the run-offs from residential lawn fertilization. If you see a well-fertilized lawn, with sprinklers going, and the water is running off onto the road and into a storm drain, that homeowner is supplying just the nutrient supply that the tiny phytoplankton plants need to grow—which, in turn, grows the tiny jellyfish, the ctenophores, which are the food source of sea nettles.

Unfortunately, where sea nettles live, they are at the top of their food chain, since the one predator of jellyfish, sea turtles, seldom venture into low salinity waters.

Thus, salinity, temperature, and nutrients are the three factors that can cause intracoastal waters to spawn sea nettles and eventually to become off limits to swimmers. But we don't have control of the salinity or temperature of these waters; our only control is over the nutrients that flow into them. It's up to all of us to be more conscientious in finally heeding the warnings which environmentalists have preached for several decades.

Winter Agitation

Winter storage decisions

For those of us who live in the higher latitudes, the approach of the fall season reminds us of an upcoming conflict between our boating agendas and the impending deep freeze. For a fortunate few, this means stowing those summer clothes on board and sailing toward warmer climates. Most of us, however, will make arrangements at the local marina for a haulout and winter cover, or possibly wet (in the water) storage. For some, who have their homes on the banks of navigable water and their boats moored at their own docks or at the community dock of a condominium, wintering their boat in the water at her normal location near home can be yet another option. This, of course, requires appropriate preparation and equipment.

One of the problems with wet storage, in latitudes where the surface of the water can freeze solid during the winter, is the potential problem of ice damage, unless proper precautions are taken.

With wooden hulls, water getting between the planks can freeze, spreading them apart and allowing more water to enter and re-freeze till a major leak and possible sinking occurs.

The problems are usually less threatening with fiberglass boats. However when thick ice forms around the hull of any boat, damage to the rudder and prop are possible. Also, when a boat is surrounded by ice, wind and current will cause it to rock and pitch. The resultant grinding action of ice against the hull can cut away at the gelcoat along the waterline of a fiberglass boat. This can result in water incursion into the laminate and, at the very least, an additional gelcoat repair job in the spring. With wooden boats, ice can wear through the paint and gouge the hull. Depending on the waterline hull shape, major structural damage can also occur. For all of these reasons it's important to prevent ice from forming around a boat that spends the winter in the water.

To make sure the boat is floating in above-freezing water, a water de-icing system in the winter is the answer. These systems are just as practical for an individual boat at a private dock as they are for a large marina. For those of us who live where the waters freeze during the winter, the "bubbler" and underwater agitation-motors are a familiar sight, but how do they keep the water from freezing around our boats?

Properties of water

Water, one of the most commonplace and familiar of all natural substances is, in fact, one of the most remarkable. Compared with nearly every other substance, water behaves, physically, in a very unique manner.

Nearly every other material expands when heated and contracts when cooled, but water follows this pattern only in part. As it is cooled down to about 39°F it does contract, but with further cooling it begins to expand again, and when it begins to freeze this expansion is dramatic.

Let's imagine what would happen if water did not follow this aberrant behavior. If water and ice continued to contract, as does nearly every other substance, ice would be denser and heavier than water. As ice formed at the cold interface of water and air, it would sink to the bottom.

Other layers of ice would also sink as they formed, until the entire body of water would be frozen solid. Since sunlight and heat don't penetrate very deeply into a body of water or ice, none of our lakes, streams and bays in the northern latitudes would ever thaw out in the summertime, except to a slight depth at the surface. Fish and nearly all forms of aquatic and bottom-life could not survive, and our northern bays, lakes and streams would be useless as a food source, for recreation, or navigation.

However when water freezes it doesn't contract, it expands, and thereby hangs an interesting scenario:

When a body of fresh water is cooled, it gradually contracts and becomes more dense and heavy until it reaches a temperature of 39°F (above freezing). Then it will begin to expand again as it is cooled down further to the freezing point and is transformed into ice (32°F or less). Although the temperatures given in these explanations are for fresh water, salt water follows a similar pattern. For salt water the exact temperatures at which these events happen are determined by the water's salinity. A solution of salt and water freezes at a lower temperature than fresh water. In fact the freezing point of a saturated solution of salt water is about -6 ° F, however the freezing point of unsaturated ocean water (depending on salinity) is around 28° F.

Since surface water that is cooled down by the cold air to 39° F becomes denser, it sinks to the bottom. It is then replaced by warmer bottom water, which then follows the same scenario. Thus no ice can ever be formed on the surface of a body of fresh water till the whole body of water is cooled to 39° F.

This means that the water at the bottom of a deep frozen lake is near 39° F whatever the temperature of the air above the ice. De-icing systems take advantage of this physical fact of nature, using this huge reservoir of warm water at the bottom for their supply of de-icing water. If we can move this relatively warmer water from the bottom to the surface around our boat, no ice can be formed in that area and we will have unfrozen water at about 39° F (4° C) surrounding the hull.

Bringing water up from the bottom

The two popular methods of raising this bottom layer of water to the surface are the air-bubbler system and the propeller-agitator.

With the air-bubbler, a weighted, perforated hose is laid along the bottom and connected to an air compressor (controlled by an air thermostat). The rising air bubbles coming out of the hose carry along with them the above-freezing water from the bottom, creating an area of unfrozen water above the bubbler hose.

The propeller-agitator accomplishes the same result by using a hermetically sealed electric motor with a propeller attached. This is lowered beneath the surface and the propeller draws the warmer water up from the bottom to accomplish the de-icing. These agitator units are also controlled by air thermostats.

Naturally, the deeper the water at the slip, the larger the reservoir of warmer water, and the more practical the de-icing system.

A bubbler system can be used equally well for an individual boat or a huge marina, with the physical size of the compressor and its horsepower dependent on the length of the bubbler hose and depth of the water. Originally these compressors were quite noisy and could be annoying in a residential environment. In recent years, however, internal as well as external sound-proofing and state-of-the-art compressor design has nearly eliminated this problem. During the winter, compressors usually live at dockside, and must be in a location well above any possible flooding.

The underwater agitation motor is completely quiet, except for the rippling noise of the water. If depth is sufficient, the underwater motor can be hung directly beneath the boat. Alternately, it can be hung at an angle off the side of the boat where the water is deepest, or at the bow facing aft. These motors can be suspended by their own ropes, mounted to a rigid arm, or suspended from a flotation unit. Most manufacturers of agitator motors have optional dock or piling mounts and flotation-mounting kits. When the underwater motors are mounted in the vertical position, these units produce a circular pattern of unfrozen water. When suspended at an angle, the pattern is elongated.

Adjusting the angle of a rope-suspended motor is done by simply looping one of the suspension ropes back one or two ribs on the propeller cage or through one of the off-center holes in the housing placed there for that purpose. These underwater motors have plastic propellers and replaccable zinc anodes for electrolysis reduction, and are available in ½, ¾ and 1 hp sizes, depending on the size of the area to be de-iced and the severity of the winters. Originally the motor cases were filled with oil, but recently synthetic dielectric lubricating fluids have been introduced that are non-toxic, biodegradable and non-bioaccumulating.

Although it would be nice if our waters were pristine, unfortunately underwater plastic bags and debris are a fact of life. If a de-icing system is used in an area where large amounts of such things are present, the chance of their fouling the propeller of an underwater motor must be taken into account when selecting a de-icing system. Naturally, underwater debris presents no problem to a bubbler system.

If needed,
an agitation motor
can be canted
at an angle

If you are using a propeller agitation system, the following practices are recommended:

1. It is usually easier to de-ice a boat by installing the de-icer at the bow and pushing the water toward the stern, since boats are designed for easiest water-flow in that direction.
2. If a boat is berthed in a river, de-icing from the upstream side will allow the current to help rather than hinder.
3. When a boat is wintering next to a bulkhead, the motor can be hung off the free side and canted toward the hull.

Obviously neither type of de-icing system can possibly prevent ice around a boat if the ice is being moved by wind or current.

Other considerations

De-icing systems are also very effective in preventing damage to pilings and docks in tidewater locations. In these locations, when ice freezes solid around a piling, the piling is frequently lifted inch by inch at each tide change. This results in expensive dock and piling repairs or replacements, come spring. Unfrozen water around the pilings can prevent this costly problem, and marinas often use bubbler systems in their slips whether or not any boats are present. This lifting, or "jacking" damage is also common in some lakes, where weather, wind, and changes in lake levels can cause the same thing to happen.

Although we only think of water agitation systems for boating use, they are also used as aeration units in fish farms. A spectacular and bizarre use of a motor-agitator made world news when, in October of 1988, whales trapped by ice at Barrow, Alaska, were kept in an ice-free area till Russian and US icebreakers could open a path for them to open water.

Even though de-icing systems eliminate most of the problems associated with wintering in the water, some other things to consider are the possibility of freezing problems inside the hull. To a large extent, the relatively warm bottom water surrounding the hull will keep the bilge free of ice, but in harsh northern climates there's no guarantee. Where electricity is available, many boat owners use electric light bulbs or small heating elements inside the engine compartment to help keep the packing glands around the prop shaft and rudder shaft, as well as the cockpit drains, from freezing.

Small, inexpensive, plug-in thermostats are also available so that the heat is not on during warm spells.

People who use a light bulb for heat can encounter several problems. A normal light bulb has a life expectancy of about 750 hours. This means that if left on continuously, it will last about a month, not nearly long enough to last through the winter. A long-life bulb, which puts out the same amount of heat, but less light, has a more rugged filament and less chance of burning out over the winter. It's also much less vulnerable to vibrations. An outdoor bulb should be used if there is any possibility of water dripping on it. The problem with light bulbs, in general, is that the very limited amount of heat generated is only effective within a very confined space and where winter temperatures are relatively mild. There have also been cases where an exposed bulb has come in contact with flammable material, or shattered and caused a fire. Marine-grade engine-compartment heaters are a far better and safer way to go. These come in several styles and wattages. Some of these heaters have their own built-in thermostat and circulating fans and are in stainless steel or aluminum cases.

Our schooner, DELPHINUS, winters in unfrozen water
at our dock on a waterway off Barnegat Bay, NJ.

Other items to check before in-the-water winter storage are the condition of your automatic bilge pump and supply of power. Is the float-switch free of debris? Can the pump be left in a standby mode without leaving the main 12-volt battery switch on for the rest of the boat? Is there a possibility of the bilge freezing, rendering the float-switch inoperable? Can the batteries remain in a charged state but not overcharged by use of a "smart" battery-charger or trickle-charger? Have you added non-toxic anti-freeze to the bilge and pumped it through the bilge-pump and discharge hoses? Other than the cockpit drains, are the through-hull seacocks closed? Ice can lift off a hose—and while you're at it, now is a good time to see if those hoses are double-clamped and the clamps and hoses are in good condition.

Even though you have done all the winterization tasks properly, an occasional mid-winter visit inside the cabin is always a good idea to make sure everything is OK—if only to assure your boat and yourself that there are warm breezes and sunny days to come. And after your check-out, a half hour curled up on the settee, with your hands wrapped around a hot cup of coffee as you plan those summer cruises, can be great therapy in relieving the depression of those cold gray days of winter as you wait for spring to creep north to reclaim the shoreline.

The Sailing Life

See How She Scoons

It is said that the name "schooner" originated when the rig first appeared on the scene, and a bystander said, "See how she scoons." Scoon is an old-time word meaning to skip across the water. It's a word seldom found in modern dictionaries.

I have had a lifetime love affair with schooners. There are still some of us, and I suspect many, who believe that no sailboat ever built can compare in beauty with the schooner. But why are people still drawn to this rig when the schooner as a recreational boat has all but faded into oblivion? I think it's because the schooner rig has a symmetrical rightness about it. With a gollywobbler, fore gaff topsail, spinnoa, flying-jib, forestaysail, fisherman—what other rig can carry such a mixed bag of sails and instead of looking ridiculous, becomes breathtaking? From the deck, as you look above, a cloud of white is overhead—but aesthetics aside, no other cruising rig has more flexibility than the schooner. It can be adjusted to suit almost any condition of wind or sea. OK, so it doesn't go to windward quite as well as that high aspect ratio IOR sloop, a characteristic common with all split rigs. But if you're searching for a love affair—if, as you sail by, you appreciate it when people turn to look and take pictures—then maybe, just maybe, you too are a schooner nut. If you are, you're in good company, since to judge by their designs and writings, John Alden, Uffa Fox, and Joseph Conrad were also schooner enthusiasts. In *Mirror of the Sea*, Conrad rhapsodized: "They are birds of the sea, whose swimming is like flying . . . the manifestation of a living creature's quick wit and graceful precision."

Although most people consider the schooner to be as American as apple pie, the popular idea that it was originated in New England is probably incorrect. It seems likely that they were first developed in Holland in the early part of the 17th century, and are depicted in paintings of that

Our schooner,
DELPHINUS

period. There's no doubt however, that America adopted the schooner as her own.

The American coastal schooners were not deliberately designed to look beautiful, they were designed as vehicles of commerce, with good carrying capacity, able to haul lumber, coal, fish, ice, stone, bricks, fertilizer and the like in all possible weather and at good speed. Thus a perfection of sail plan and hull was developed, and something completely functional as well as aesthetically beautiful was the result. They were as vital to U.S. commerce as are the highways, railroads and airlines of today. In the days before the railroads, when overland routes were not much more than muddy paths in the warm months and snow-covered ruts during the winter, the coastal schooner moved people and supplies between the coastal cities.

Waterborne commerce along the east coast of the United States was a natural result of its topography. Our eastern shoreline is replete with estuaries, rivers, bays, and sounds, which allowed the windward ability of the schooner to carry them far inland where square-riggers dared not venture. By the late 18th century, the schooner had become the national sailboat of the US and replaced the square-rigger as the ship of choice for coastal commerce.

During the schooners' heyday boat builders all up and down the coast were trying to keep up with the demand and were turning out large coastal schooners in record numbers. The town of Camden, Maine alone sent over 200 down the ways, and vintage schooners can still be seen in New England harbors.

Even though the coastal schooner was a boon to commerce, by today's standards travel in those days was still primitive. A trip from New York to Philadelphia, which now takes about two hours by car, would take 2 days by coastal schooner if the wind was exactly right, or could take two weeks under adverse conditions—and there was always the possibility of never arriving at all if a nor'easter reared up offshore.

But exactly what constitutes this rig that transformed the early days of our nation? The schooner is characterized by fore-and-aft sails, set on two or more masts, the foremast(s) being equal in height to, or shorter, than the mainmast, which is the farthest aft. Some early schooners were rigged with square sails on the forward mast, and were known as topsail schooners.

The schooner rig has three basic types of sailplans: The old-time gaff main and gaff foresail, the Marconi main and gaff foresail (which allows a permanent backstay on the mainmast, by use of a boomkin), and the Marconi main with a staysail in place of the foresail. The fishing schooners of the 19th and early 20th centuries usually carried three headsails: jib, jib staysail, and jib topsail, but most small schooners of today opt for a single headsail for ease in handling. When this headsail is on a boom it doesn't even have to be tended when coming-about. (For a more detailed description, see *The Club-Footed Jib* in the *Sails and Rigging* section of this book).

There are some sails that are indigenous only to schooners. The gollywobbler is the schooner's version of a spinnaker. It's a huge staysail, usually bigger than the main and foresail combined, and is set in place of them for downwind running. It does, however, require a large crew to handle it, and is seldom seen today. The fisherman staysail, still frequently used on even the smallest of schooners, is a trapezoidal sail that fills the area between the tops of the mainmast and foremast. It is hoisted by its own halyards to the tops of these masts and, depending on the tack, can either be on the windward or leeward side of the foresail. Although the fisherman's staysail is seemingly archaic, designer Ted Brewer says, "It's even more efficient than a genoa when going to windward."

The flexibility of the schooner rig to meet a variety of conditions is its greatest asset. When the wind starts to blow a gale, the schooner can begin by dropping one of its auxiliary sails, such as the fisherman. This can be followed by putting in reefs on the mainsail and/or foresail. Higher winds can be countered by dropping the foresail, and maintaining a balance under jib and mainsail alone. Under really severe conditions, the schooner can continue under double-reefed foresail alone, or heave-to under foresail. The feeling of proceeding under reefed foresail or heaving-to under reefed foresail was so confidence-inspiring that when weathering a storm out on the Grand Banks under reefed foresail the Gloucester fishermen described it as being in "foresail harbor."

On downwind runs the schooner can wing-and-wing the sails, with the mainsail out to one side and the foresail on the other, presenting a huge sail area. Old time schooner captains called this "reading the book," since the configuration replicated the pages of an open book; and on rare occasions, when the wind was light and the seas calm, I've been able to sail my schooner downwind with everything up (jib, foresail, fisherman and mainsail), sailing wing-and-wing-and-wing-and-wing.

When a modern-day sailor first goes aboard a schooner, it is daunting to say the least—there seem to be lines everywhere. On our modest-sized schooner, the running rigging, proceeding from bow to stern, consists of: jib halyard, jib downhaul, jib sheet, jib-boom lazyjacks, fisherman-staysail halyard (and when hoisted, the fisherman staysail tack downhaul), gaff foresail throat halyard, gaff foresail peak halyard, foresail boom vang, foresail gaff vang, foresail lazyjacks, fisherman staysail peak halyard (and when hoisted, the fisherman port and starboard sheets), centerboard pendant, main boom topping lift, main halyard, main boom vang, mast-top flag halyard, spreader flag halyard, main lazyjacks and main sheet.

This is an intimidating array for the newcomer on board, but those lines are there to make the job easier, and once you "learn the ropes," sailing a schooner shorthanded or singlehanded can be easier than sailing a sloop of comparable sail area, since, with this split rig, each of the sails is smaller and easier to manage. I singlehand my schooner most of the time, even when there are guests aboard, and find it easier than a sloop of comparable size.

Unfortunately, anyone looking for a schooner today has limited choices. In the used boat market there are always some wooden hulls available, and occasionally ones of steel or aluminum, but fiberglass-hulled schooners are harder to come by. For about 25 years, the Lazy Jack 32 was available to the small-boat sailor. This schooner, designed by Ted Brewer and made in fiberglass by Ted Hermann Boats of Southold, NY, is 32 feet on deck and 39 feet overall, including the bowsprit and boomkin. It was available as either a bare hull, kit, or completed boat; but in 1987, with Ted's retirement, production ceased and the mold was destroyed.

Then Cherubini Boat Company decided to resurrect this small schooner as one of their own, and a mold was re-cast from an existing hull. Cherubini is well-acquainted with the schooner rig. For years they have been producing the semi-custom Cherubini 48 fiberglass schooner out of their plant in New

Jersey. This is a gorgeous boat, with traditional line, a saucy shear, tumble-home, and varnished teak, along with the beautiful schooner sailplan. This is the only company I know of now building fiberglass schooners.

Just over 20 years ago, the lodestone force of the schooner finally became irresistible and we started hunting for a design that would meet our needs. We wanted a boat that would be practical for cruises along the East and Gulf coasts, using both offshore and inland waters. This meant shoal draft but with self-righting design and an easily handled rig on a hull size big enough to provide comfortable liveaboard accommodations, yet small enough to be easily sailed by one person with a minimum requirement of physical strength. A snappy appearance wouldn't hurt either.

After a long search through hundreds of designs that all fell just a little short of our dreamboat, we ran across an old brochure of the Ted Brewer-designed Lazy Jack Schooner, whose graceful fiberglass hull is a modern scaled-down version of a small coastal schooner of the 19th century. The instant I saw the plans I knew that this was our boat.

I've built several small boats in the past and I wanted to complete this boat myself, from a bare hull. This would allow me to put in all the features that I wanted, based on the 17 boats I've owned over the past 65 years. The builder, Ted Hermann, agreed to have a bare hull laid up for us and also offered his expertise. He also supplied specialized fittings such as those for the bowsprit, boomkin, rudder heel-plate and centerboard. He had patterns of all the various wood sections which we could trace, and when it came time, he lent us a short section of mast extrusion, so that, for our two keel-stepped masts, the deck holes and mast-step fittings could be installed and aligned well before the real masts would be stepped in place.

Brewer's keel/centerboard design was ideal for the waters of the Intracoastal Waterway, and the keel/centerboard draft of three feet with the board up provides many gunkholing opportunities. And, although shoal-draft, she is stiff. It wasn't until the second year after completing our boat that, in near-gale winds, with everything up, and with deliberate intent, my son and I finally managed to get the rail wet.

Most modern-day sailors looking at our schooner think it's too complicated and probably slow, but nothing could be further from the truth. Remember, those Gloucester fishing schooners evolved from a requirement of speed and seaworthiness, and for most of the 20th century the fastest Atlantic Ocean crossing for a monohull was held by the schooner ATLANTIC, which won the Transatlantic Kaiser's Cup Race of 1905.

Our schooner's rig offers an almost unlimited variety of sail combinations to meet any condition of wind or weather, yet, except when our fisherman's staysail is flying, all our sails are self-tending. Coming about merely involves turning the wheel and watching as first the club-footed jib, then the foresail and finally the mainsail swing over to the new tack. It makes you feels slightly guilty, as if you should be doing something. Although an overlapping jib would mean more sail area and a better slot, it would also mean frantically dragging the sail around and winching it in during each change of tack, another task we've eliminated.

The lack of sheet and halyard winches aboard attests to the modest strength requirements necessary. In lieu of winches, multiple-part block and tackle provides the mechanical advantage, as it did in the old fishing schooners.

Lazyjacks are used on all three sails for easier control when lowering sail single-handed, and the jib and foresail lazyjacks also serve the dual purpose of topping lifts. A jib downhaul line pulls the jib down from a safe place on the foredeck, and a boom gallows for the main locks the boom in place for easy furling in a seaway. This boom gallows also makes the boom a firm ridgepole for a cockpit cover on rainy days or a hammock on sunny ones.

Our inboard power consists of a Yanmar diesel, pushing a three-blade prop.

Permanent, folding mast-steps, leading to the top of each mast, provide secure footing and eliminate hoisting your mate up on a bosun's chair for rigging changes, repairs, inspections, or to retrieve that lost halyard. And on the foredeck an electric anchor winch helps ease the strain on our old backs.

Our navigational gear consists of a magnetic compass, Loran (which uses our insulated backstay as the antenna), and a GPS chart plotter. A Benmar autopilot, out of sight in the lazarette, is coupled by chain-drive to the steering shaft. VHF, CB and FRS radios, depth sounder, hand-bearing compass and sextant complete the inventory.

On deck we have teak accessories: rails, bowsprit, boomkin, hatch doors, belaying-pin racks (yes, we do have belaying pins), and blocks, giving added warmth and a traditional look. All eleven bronze ports open, and the forward hatch opens in either direction.

The interior is finished in varnished mahogany, and between the mahogany and the fiberglass hull are panels of polyurethane insulation, covered with aluminum foil. The insulation provides more interior comfort and eliminates sweating, and the insulation's foil covering provides the added benefit of creating a good radar return blip to other boats. Our interior accommodations include an Isotherm 12-volt refrigerator/freezer using a eutectic holding plate, three different cabin heaters: a diesel cabin heater; a bulkhead-mounted electric heater (using dockside power); and a heater that works from the engine's coolant. We have a hot and cold pressure water system which works from either 12 volts or by using a single foot-pump at each location. The hot water is supplied by either dock power or from an engine heat-exchanger. There's a saltwater tap at the galley sink for dishwashing and fresh water conservation, and hot and cold water showers in the head and cockpit. We have both electric and kerosene cabin lights, and for entertainment we have AM, FM, cassette, and CD, as well as a 12-volt TV (antenna on the foremast). Our marine air conditioner uses a saltwater heat exchanger, is tucked under the settee and runs off shore power for those hot, humid, windless nights in a marina.

First mate Elsie is a gourmet cook and excellent meals aboard have always ranked high on our list. Our stainless steel, kerosene, gimbaled, three-burner stove and oven, and a small microwave oven, help provide these meals (our very first meal on board, after the stove was installed, was Cornish game hens). In a marina, with dock power, a Formica countertop slides over the stove, and an electric hotplate or toaster-oven on this countertop is frequently enough to supply our needs, as well as reducing unwanted heat during mealtime.

To supply AC power for the microwave, power tools, hair dryer, etc., we have a 2000-watt inverter. When it is turned on, all the AC outlets on board are changed over to the inverter output through a DPDT relay which, in its at-rest position, connects these outlets to the shore power inlet receptacle.

As with most cruising sailboats, we consider a reliable and convenient dinghy an absolute must. When anchored out or at a mooring, it's our transportation to and from shore and neighboring boats. We tried an inflatable for several years, but were frustrated with its skittish behavior, set-up time, its susceptibility to abrasion and puncturing at dockside or when beaching, and its poor rowing qualities. We much prefer a hard dinghy. So when taking an intracoastal trip, or when coastal cruising we often tow our Bauer-10 dinghy—a beautifully-designed boat that's great for rowing, motoring or sailing. If we expect to be sailing offshore, however, we don't want a dinghy in tow, and we take along an eight-foot folding dinghy. The one we have is an English boat. It is made from ¼" marine mahogany plywood and folds up to 4" thick. It lives on deck in its vinyl storage bag between the two masts. When unfolded, we hoist it over the side using the two fisherman's halyards (on the foremast and mainmast)—a near duplication of the launching method the Gloucester fishing schooners used to launch their dories. If we will be leaving the boat for any length of time, we stow our folding dinghy in the main cabin, a rather unusual concept for a hard dinghy, but one of complete practicality. It's an ideal deterrent to those who might want to "borrow" it.

So, after several years of planning and work, our boat has turned out just as we hoped. I don't advocate this design for everyone, but for us it's perfect. We have an able, comfortable and manageable boat with the beautiful and traditional lines of the romantic schooner era. Our schooner, DELPHINUS, has been a family member for nearly three decades now. Since we are now in our 80s, ease of singlehanding our boat is a prime requisite, and our schooner fills the bill. Another peripheral advantage of our schooner rig is when anchoring under sail. We can approach a crowded anchorage with everything up, select our spot, come up into the wind and sheet the mainsail in tight amidships. Since the mainsail is so far aft, this keeps us neatly weathervaned into the wind while we leisurely drop the jib and lower the anchor as we begin to fall back. Then the fisherman, foresail, and finally the mainsail can be dropped in a relaxed manner while at anchor.

DELPHINUS whose name is Latin for dolphin and the constellation of the dolphin, sports a carved teak figurehead of a jumping dolphin beneath her bowsprit. It serves not only as a decorative appendage, but also as a bowsprit brace. It's a great hit both on the water and at dockside, and seems to be a special attraction to children. As enlightened sailors, we know that our figurehead is purely decorative—and yet, sometimes there's the feeling of a "presence" at our bow, guiding us through unfamiliar waters.

With our cruising schooner we feel quite content. We have an able, comfortable and manageable boat with the beautiful and traditional lines of the schooner era—but our boat is ours in more than the ordinary sense of ownership. It is ours because built into it are small parts of ourselves; the planning, work, sweat, skinned knuckles, and bruised knees, along with our love of the schooner rig. All are hidden in the dark crevices of the hull, as much a part of our schooner as the bowsprit and boomkin. Possession like that is hard to come by, it can't be bought, it must be earned.

So in choosing a sailboat, its ultimate windward ability is not the only thing to consider, the owners must also take pride in their craft. Beauty and practicality *can* coexist. In our advanced years it's satisfying to know that there are some things that *do* improve with age: old wine to drink, old friends to talk to, old authors to read, and old sailboat designs to admire and enjoy.

Sailing Into Old Age

If you remember when all sailboats were made of wood, with manila lines, galvanized fittings, cotton sails, and wood spars, chances are you have discovered that growing old is the most unexpected thing that happens in your lifetime. With that three-score milestone in your wake, sailing priorities change.

I've been sailing for over 73 years, and my wife, Elsie, for 56 years (ever since we were married). We've sailed in all types and sizes of craft and, if the fates allow, look forward to many more years on the water. But why sail at our age when we can stay in the non-threatening security of a home ashore? Of course security is admirable, but it's only one aspect of our existence—we must also have things to challenge us, to excite us—things to work at, and thus enhance the fabric of our lives. What are the special problems for the over-the-hill gang who want to stay on the water, but would like to take things a little easier and enjoy a little more comfort?

The simplistic answer is to switch to a smaller boat or change from a sailboat to a trawler-type powerboat. For ease of handling, it would be ideal to have the smallest sailboat that meets your needs, within the boundaries of safety, comfort and enjoyment. But that misses the point. Undoubtedly by now those sailors in their 60s, 70s, or 80s have the type of boat they love, fitted out with all the things that make it home, and renouncing their love and embarking on a new boating relationship is not an enticing thought. But we're not as able-bodied as we used to be—a hard thing to admit. Handling a large boat, climbing in and out of dinghies, sore muscles or a bad back, moving about in rough weather, raising and lowering sail, or hauling in the anchor—all become unexpectedly taxing. I enjoy singlehanding my boat, and I have my solo deckwork routine down pat; but I must admit that I've had a couple of bad scares on deck that I haven't mentioned to my wife. So lately I've been taking more time to think out my deck work, and I prepare more carefully while solo sailing. Although sailing my boat takes lots of work, giving up my schooner would be like asking me to reject one of our children.

Reducing the physical requirements of deck work

There are several generalities that apply across the board for the older sailor. Reduction in physical requirements is primary. For nearly every physically taxing job on deck, there is an easier way, or a piece of equipment that can reduce the muscle-power and agility required.

When anchoring, do you have to hand the anchor over the side? If so, is it possible to install a roller on the bow where a plow anchor can be stowed? If you use a fluke-type anchor, how about changing from one of the heavy galvanized-steel ones to one of the light weight modern aluminum-alloy types? Along with a reduction in weight, you can actually increase your holding power. The pull required to release an anchor from a sticky mud bottom is daunting for the older back. An electric or mechanical anchor-winch can be a great asset—and when that winch can be operated from the cockpit, anchoring becomes even simpler.

You have probably used safety lines in the past, but use them more frequently now, especially when you're alone on deck. Remember, those reaction times have slowed down some. If you have no fore-and-aft safety lines, or jacklines, the installation process is not that complicated, and the small expense involved is a good insurance policy. Forged padeyes, through-bolted with backing plates, mounted fore and aft and connected with wire or nylon line, constitute the safety lines. When choosing the safety-line material, consider using flat nylon webbing in place of the usual round lines, since the round ones tend to roll underfoot and could cause a fall. If they are installed free of obstructions, your safety harness can be clipped on in the cockpit and you can travel from cockpit to bow without unclipping. Some people use two lengths of clip-on lines on their harness, the longer one allowing foredeck work. Our schooner sports a long bowsprit. Although it gives a saucy look, it presents special problems for a safety line. To solve this we use our fisherman-staysail halyard (which goes to the top of the foremast, near the bow), which is cleated off at a pre-marked position, to which our harness is clipped when doing work out on the end of the bowsprit.

And if the ultimate happens, and someone goes overboard, a man-overboard retrieval system should be easily available on deck. We have a Lifesling, fastened to our stern boom-gallows. But what if you go overboard while solo? A lifejacket (I wear an inflatable one) and a line trailing astern

Mast steps make it easy to go aloft, and provide a secure footing. Note the lineman's belt going around the mast, which would catch on a mast step in an emergency

are good ideas. But can you get back on deck when you're next to the boat? We have a rope ladder with hard rungs that remains on deck, fastened to the base of one of the stanchions. A ⅛" nylon line from the bottom rung hangs over the side of the boat, and can be reached from the water. I'd like to say I've never had to use it, but once I went into the drink when getting into my dinghy while at anchor in a secluded cove. It worked out very nicely (and there was no one around to see my foolishness).

Trips to the top of the mast are usually not something sailors look forward to, and for older sailors this can become particularly daunting. I've installed folding mast steps to the top of both our mainmast and foremast. This lets me go up the mast on my own, and at my own pace, without the need of someone on deck hoisting me. The folding steps give a good, solid feeling of stability, lacking in many of the other mast-climbing methods. When climbing the mast I always use a nylon linesman's belt, which keeps me completely safe while climbing and when aloft.

Much fatiguing and hazardous foredeck work can be reduced with a jib-furling system. Aside from its obvious advantages, it makes the foredeck a safer place when anchoring under sail, with no sailcloth or sheets to slide on or trip over. It also provides a genoa which is stored on a furling system and not taking up room in the cabin or sail-locker.

To ease mainsail furling, lazyjacks will hold the sail close to the boom when lowered. This helps prevent the lowered sail from billowing out in the wind, getting underfoot, or blocking visibility. They are easily rigged with a minimum of hardware. Their only two drawbacks are a slight increase in windage aloft, and the added care when hoisting sail—that is, keeping the battens from going outside the lazyjacks. The lazyjacks also provide an emergency back-up system in the event of a topping-lift failure, preventing the boom from dropping into the cockpit and doing damage to equipment or craniums. Of course a roller-furling system on the mainsail is another way of simplifying the furling procedure and should be considered when purchasing a new boat, but for an existing boat it will mean major re-fitting and expense.

Our traditionally-rigged schooner has a boom gallows, another asset to ease sail-furling. Although I never had a boat with one before, it seems ready-made for the older sailor. When furling the main in high and confused seas, while standing on the cockpit seats, we now have a solid boom to hang on to, instead of one that is swinging back and forth, trying to throw us out of the cockpit. An ancillary advantage of the boom gallows is that it provides a stable ridge-pole for a boom tent, or cockpit awning.

And speaking of cockpit awnings, we all know that reducing our amount of time in the sun is essential. Although this advice is true for all age groups, it's only as we get older that those sun-worshipping indiscretions of our youth are returning to haunt us and we are belatedly concerned. A wide-brimmed hat is a good idea, and make sure when purchasing sunglasses that they are UV 400-protected. Our eyes have been subjected to a lifetime of sunlight but it's not too late to give them better care. In addition to the hat and sunblock, a cockpit dodger, awning, or bimini will not only reduce the UV, but make the cockpit more enjoyable in hot climates—as well as on rainy days. We have a cockpit awning that fastens onto the aft edge of our fiberglass dodger with a boltrope and track (see *Boltrope it On* in the *Sails and Rigging* chapter of this book) and extends back to our boom gallows. It has two side panels that can be attached to the lifelines, which keeps the rain outside of the cockpit coaming. Although the mainsail can't be used when the awning is in place, it is wonderful while at anchor, in a marina, or while motoring on a rainy day.

If you don't have one already, consider an autopilot. There are many good ones on the market which, for a very small investment of electricity, will save many tedious hours at the helm. They are also a delight when hoisting sail singlehanded, holding you into the wind perfectly and obviating those mad dashes back into the cockpit to readjust your heading. Autopilots are also especially welcome on those long days under power when the engine is providing the necessary electricity.

Another aid to hoisting sail singlehanded is by leading halyards back to winches in the cockpit where you are close to your engine and rudder controls.

The dinghy becomes unexpectedly heavier as we get older. Stern davits ease its handling. If you prefer a hard dinghy, you might want to consider a nesting dinghy which allows you to lower smaller and lighter sections over the side from the cabin top, or a folding dinghy. When we are cruising offshore we keep a wooden eight-foot folding dinghy on deck. With its four-inch thickness when folded, it doesn't hamper visibility.

Are the soles of those comfortable old deck shoes becoming hard and slippery? Relegate them to shoreside activities. A few splashes of bottom paint won't hurt them now. You don't want to become the new candidate for the "I've fallen and I can't get up" commercial.

Being in the cockpit during those cold, windy days in the spring or fall, can be exhausting. A dodger provides protection from the cold wind and spray. And to make the trip to the foredeck around the dodger safer, we've installed dodger handholds. Weather cloths, fastened to the deck stanchions, also help to cut those chilling winds.

Adding to comfort belowdeck

Although safety equipment and labor-saving devices on deck are important, let's not forget life belowdeck.

It's a paradox that the older we get, the more we want to simplify our lives, and at the same time, the more comfort counts. In pursuit of the comfort side of the equation, an inverter that will power a small microwave, hair dryer, or electric coffeepot, can make your sailing life easier. In the last year or two inverter sizes and prices have come down and their AC output wattages and efficiencies have gone up. However, it's a good idea to run the engine whenever the inverter is supplying a heavy load for an extended time.

I've noticed that as I get older, high heat and humidity, as well as cold windy days, become more intolerable. For those hot, humid, uncomfortable, windless days in a marina, we've installed a small marine air conditioner (with saltwater heat-exchanger) beneath the settee. A few years ago we were visiting a marina in Baltimore's Inner Harbor in August. It was 90 degrees with 90% humidity, and not a breath of air. Our on-board air conditioner was a lifesaver for a good night's sleep.

The flip side of this is a way of heating the cabin on cold nights. Deciding on which heating system to install is not an easy one. Price, size, reliability, safety, ease of maintenance and installation, combustion efficiency, heat-exchanger efficiency, choice of hot water, forced air, convection, electric, propane, compressed natural gas, diesel, or kerosene, are options to evaluate. (See: *Cabin Heaters* in the *In the Cabin* section of this book). We have three kerosene lamps aboard, a trawler lamp above the cabin table and two bulkhead-mounted ones. These do nicely to take the chill off on a cool evening, but for really cold weather, our diesel cabin heater will bring the cabin temperature up into the seventies on the coldest of nights. When in a marina on a cold night, we have an electric heater that we use, when ample shorepower is available, and when motoring our engine supplies the hot water for our automotive-type heater. If you're using any type of flame to heat the cabin, or if you have a cooking stove that uses a combustible fuel, investing in a 12-volt carbon-monoxide detector is a must. It's a good investment in any case, since it can also warn you of engine exhaust problems.

When installing labor-saving devices and amenities, remember the old engineering truism: "As the complexity of a system approaches infinity, the time between failures approaches zero." This means that you should have manuals aboard for all your equipment, and if your technical abilities preclude repairing them, then taking them out of service, bypassing them, or changing to a simpler system, should be in your bag of tricks.

Do you need some extra handholds in the cabin? They are a good day's project that will repay your efforts sometime in the future.

As important as it is to upgrade your boat's hardware, remember that your mental software may also need some reprogramming. When on a cruise, if the weather is kicking up and you're secure at anchor, on a mooring, or in a marina, a day of boatkeeping might be more productive than fighting it out outside. There are always those little jobs to be done. When was the last time you changed your oil?

And if you're coastal cruising, plan on shorter day's runs, you'll enjoy the cruise more if you're not pushing your limits.

Also, try and resist the temptation, when sailing on the same course as another sailboat, to engage in a race. You're not in the business of having to prove yourself every day anymore.

It's also a good idea to pay attention to the old adage: "The time to shorten sail is when you first begin to think about it." The corollary to this is carrying less sail to begin with. After all, it's easier to cook and move about when you're at a reasonable angle of heel.

Attitude

Perhaps it's the hardening realization of mortality, but I've found that my appreciation of a life afloat actually seems heightened as I grow older.

I see cruising under sail as a metaphor of our lives. We hone our skills and start out for destinations we hope to reach, and may never reach, and if we do, it may be much later than we intended. There are unexpected storms along the way, forcing us to change our plans, and sometimes taking us to places more fascinating and encounters more exciting than those we had originally envisioned. But by the grace of God, good luck, perseverance, and an accident of genes, we've made it this far in reasonably good health and agility. However that doesn't warrant any special consideration or veneration from others. As another old sailor would say at the end of his nightly newscasts, "That's the way it is."

For me, the most satisfying part of being on a small boat is the sense of self-sufficiency with its subdivisions, ingenuity and endurance. These elements can be minor, almost trivial, the seriousness of the problem has nothing to do with this special feeling of independence, this last vestige of a place in the world where neither government nor social status can help—or interfere. You can be on your own partly or entirely, depending on how much self-sufficiency you feel like taking on. For those of any age, it's a matter of feeling alive.

Index

INDEX

About the Author

Donald Launer has always had a love affair with small boats, designing and building his first boat when he was eleven years old. Nearly thirty years ago he obtained a commercial Coast Guard Captain's License and began writing for recreational boating magazines.

Captain Launer has cruised the east coast from Canada to Key West, the Bahamas, Virgin Islands, and Mediterranean, writing about these cruises in international, national and regional periodicals: *Cruising World, Offshore, SAIL, Soundings, Chesapeake Bay Magazine, Coastal Cruising, and NJ Waterways.* He has been co-contributor for several nautical books, and has had his own column in *The Beachcomber.* For 15 years he was the Field Editor for the yearly *Waterway Guide,* and he is currently contributing editor for *Good Old Boat Magazine.* His book, *A Cruising Guide to New Jersey Waters* (the only book dealing exclusively with New Jersey's navigable waters) was published in hard-cover by Rutgers University Press in 1995 and is now in paperback in its second printing. The completely revised 2nd Edition came out in May 2004. His last book was a reference book, titled, *Dictionary of Nautical Acronyms and Abbreviations,* and was also published by Sheridan House.

Captain Launer has owned over 18 boats, many of which he built himself. He built his schooner, DELPHINUS, from a bare hull, and it is berthed next to his home on Barnegat Bay on the New Jersey shore.